ROOTS, RULES AND TRIBULATION

ROOTS, RULES AND TRIBULATION
Andrew Bethell

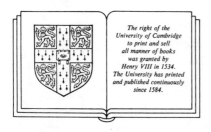

The right of the
University of Cambridge
to print and sell
all manner of books
was granted by
Henry VIII in 1534.
The University has printed
and published continuously
since 1584.

Cambridge University Press

CAMBRIDGE
LONDON   NEW YORK   NEW ROCHELLE
MELBOURNE   SYDNEY

ACT NOW PLAYS

Series editor: Andrew Bethell

Roots, Rules and Tribulation Andrew Bethell
Closed Circuit Mike English
Faust and Furious Anne Lee
Czechmate Gerry Docherty and Bill Kinross
Spring Offensive Ray Speakman and Derek Nicholls
Football Apprentices David Holman
Gregory's Girl Bill Forsyth
Vacuees Bill Martin

Published by the Press Syndicate of the University of Cambridge
The Pitt Building, Trumpington Street, Cambridge CB2 1RP
32 East 57th Street, New York, NY 10022, USA
10 Stamford Road, Oakleigh, Melbourne 3166, Australia

© Cambridge University Press

First published 1982
Third printing 1984

Printed in Great Britain by David Green Printers Ltd.

British Library cataloguing in publication data

Bethell, Andrew
Roots, rules and tribulations—(Act now)
I. Title II. Series
822^1 .914   PR6052.E8/
ISBN 0 521 28570 4

Performance
For permission to give a public performance of *Roots, Rules and Tribulation* please write to Permissions Department, Cambridge University Press, The Edinburgh Building, Shaftesbury Road, Cambridge CB2 2RU.

ABOUT THE PLAY

We hear a lot nowadays about the best way to deal with juvenile crime. Punishment is back in fashion; the short, sharp shock, we are told, will teach young hooligans a lesson. Or will it?

Roots, Rules and Tribulation is about six young offenders, three boys and three girls, whose crimes range from shoplifting in Oxford Street to assault on the common. Instead of being sent to Borstal or a detention centre, the six offenders have been sentenced to work on a community service scheme and are given jobs as gardeners in the municipal park - a punishment which the loud-mouthed park keeper calls the 'soft option'.

In the park, the offenders come into contact with a rich variety of characters and attitudes: truanting schoolboys who steal bikes for a laugh, three would-be Rastafarians who are picked up by the police on suspicion, and an old woman tramp who has seen better times.

The play follows the fortunes of the offenders as they finish their sentences and go their separate ways, while a new group of offenders takes their place. There are no easy answers in the play; some of the characters find success of a sort, while for others the problems of living are still too difficult to handle.

Roots, Rules and Tribulation raises important questions in a way that young people will find instantly recognisable as well as enjoyable. The play was specially commissioned by the Cockpit Theatre and Arts Workshop, and was produced by the Cockpit Youth Theatre in 1979, directed by Ian Brown.

CHARACTERS

Male

NIGEL BARROWS   the assistant park keeper

ALF SPRATCHETT   the park keeper

THE MAN IN THE BLACK COAT

REG JARVIS   the parks gardener

PETE   a young offender

CARLTON   a young offender, a West Indian

SIDNEY   a young offender

NORRIS   West Indian youth

WENDELL   West Indian youth

SYLVAN   West Indian youth

POLICEMAN   (PC)

DONALD   a jogger

KEVIN   a truant

LEN   a truant

BRIAN   a truant

Female

MRS WALTON   a mother

JO   a young offender

ARLENE   a young offender

DENISE   a young offender

SUSIE   an office worker

POLICEWOMAN   (WPC)

ETHEL   a tramp

MAGGIE   a community care officer

DOREEN   a West Indian girl

SONIA   a West Indian girl, Mrs Walton's daughter

A TEACHER

STAGE DIRECTIONS

There are two kinds of directions in this playscript. Those in **bold type** provide information that is essential to an understanding of what is happening in the play at that time. For a play-reading, these should be read by a separate reader.

Those in *italic type* are less essential stage directions and offer suggestions to assist with a production of the play on stage. In a reading they are best not read out as they will hamper the flow of the play, although those who are reading may find that some of these instructions offer help with the interpretation of their lines.

ACT ONE

SCENE 1   A municipal park in March. Two flower beds, empty. A patch of grass covered with the litter of a Sunday afternoon. Two park benches and a litter basket. The junction of several paths. It is early Monday morning. Sounds of birds and traffic.

(THE MAN IN THE BLACK COAT walks on with a slow despair. He carries a newspaper – he sits on a bench. Reads briefly. He is disturbed, turns the pages with increasing disgust. Gets up and violently and viciously kicks litter bin over onto the grass. He walks off. Enter NIGEL BARROWS, an assistant park keeper in his twenties. He wears the park keeper's brown in a casual style. He carries a litter prong and a bag. His heart is not in the job. He tries a few different styles with the litter prong . . . a golfer, a polo player, etc.)

MRS WALTON   *(Off stage)* Selwyn! Selwyn, where are you? Selwyn, will you come back now!

(Enter MRS WALTON, a middle-aged West Indian woman. She carries a Tesco bag. She has obviously just rushed out of the house. She wears slippers and a housecoat.)

Selwyn! *(She sees Nigel.)* Excuse me Mr Park Keeper, sir. Have you seen a young black boy come by here just now?

NIGEL   Reading a comic?

MRS WALTON   Most likely.

NIGEL   He passed me a few minutes ago. Anything wrong?

MRS WALTON   His daddy gonna inflate 'is backside when he get 'ome. Hey, there he is, goin' outta the gate. Here Selwyn, you come back here, I tell you . . . (She goes off.)
(Nigel sees the litter bin.)

NIGEL   Vandals. *(He wearily replaces the litter.)*

(He spots a half-eaten fish and chip dinner. He lapses back into his fantasy, this time as a matador. With much posturing and trumpet calls he approaches the rubbish and executes a deft blow.)

Hey Toro!

(Meanwhile a girl, SUSIE, clearly on her way to work, has been watching with some amusement and then, well aware of the embarrassment she will cause, strides past jauntily.)

SUSIE   Lovely morning!

NIGEL   Uh . . . yes . . . yes it is.

SUSIE   Soon be spring.

NIGEL   Soon will be . . .

(Exit Susie. Nigel stares after her in appreciation and acute embarrassment.) . . . spring, oh God! *(He lapses into silence.)* No . . . no . . . no . . . I'm only filling in for a friend . . . he's off sick . . . yes . . . spiked his foot . . . went septic . . . No, no! He's getting better all the time . . . Well, I usually . . . I mean, I'm between jobs . . . you know how it is . . . Oh, are you? . . . sounds marvellous . . . I like the sound of that. Perhaps I could pick you up . . . Oh, you've got a flat of your own? Sounds perfect . . . about eight . . .

(Enter SPRATCHETT, the park keeper. He wears his brown suit like a uniform and moves and talks like an ex-corporal, which he is. He has listened to Nigel's fantasy - but ignores the possibilities for banter.)

SPRATCHETT   You're late!

NIGEL   No I'm not. I've been picking litter since eight.

SPRATCHETT   You've not fed the ducks or cleared the bins and it's almost nine. It's slackness.

NIGEL   But there's much more than usual and this bin . . .

SPRATCHETT   You don't have to tell me, sonny Jim. Just read the papers.

NIGEL   The litter, I meant the litter. There's more than usual.

SPRATCHETT   It's all the same. No one cares any more. Can't be bothered you see. They just can't be bothered. When I was in Malacca, the RSM used to put 'em in heavy fatigues and double them through the jungle, just for leaving a toffee paper on the parade ground.

NIGEL   I can't see it working now.

(Enter MAGGIE, a probation officer. She is in her middle twenties. She carries a clip board.)

SPRATCHETT   'Course you can't that's just the trouble. National Service then, gave them a good dose of discipline just when they needed it. Gave the young a bit of spine, a bit of backbone . . .

MAGGIE   Mr Spratchett, is it?

SPRATCHETT   Yes, that's me, and what can I do for you, young lady?

MAGGIE   I've come from the community home.

SPRATCHETT   Oh gawd, the Borstal boys. I'd almost forgotten. Was it today? Must have been. Slipped my mind. Nigel, you should have reminded me.

MAGGIE   Yes, you said you could use six, on the Additional Seasonal Labour Scheme. And they're not . . .

SPRATCHETT   Did I say six?

MAGGIE   Yes, it says six here to help in the gardens, and Mr Spratchett, I ought to explain they're not Borstal boys.

SPRATCHETT   Don't tell me! We are not supposed to call it Borstal any more are we? It's that fancy new place down Church Street. Looks more like a holiday camp than a prison.

MAGGIE   Well it's not Borstal exactly. It's an experimental community home. All the young people have committed offences which would usually put them away in a remand home, but we're trying to offer them a more positive alternative. They come to us and as soon as we think they're ready we send them out on community service projects, on trust.

SPRATCHETT   Don't tell me. Don't tell me, I've heard it all before. The soft option, an easy number. Try to understand their childhood problems too, I suppose.

MAGGIE   Yes, that's one part of it. You could put it like that. Many of them do need help in sorting out why they feel the way they do.

SPRATCHETT   Help! Tell that to the old ladies they left for dead. They're the ones that need help, my girl, the victims. I know that doesn't fit in with what they told you at university, but it is the victim that needs the holiday camp and the understanding. The young thugs need punishing. How else are you going to put a stop to it, eh? Tell me that.

MAGGIE   Of course the victims need help, but simple punishment may make us feel better, but it doesn't solve anything. It usually breeds mistrust and a violent response and so we're back where we started.

SPRATCHETT   People can't walk the streets for fear of these young hooligans, and you're worried about mistrust. I'm sorry to laugh, young lady, but you've got a nerve, at your age telling me about trust. I remember what it was like round here before you were even thought of. A community it was then, we didn't even lock our doors. Every home was a community home.

MAGGIE   That's not quite what I've been told. Social conditions in London before the war . . .

SPRATCHETT   Social conditions. Don't talk to me about social conditions. We didn't even know about them in those days. We may have been poor but we were happy. Every man, woman and child.

MAGGIE   Well that's as may be.

SPRATCHETT   Ha, got no answer to that have you?

MAGGIE   I think I might have, but I haven't got time to hang around here arguing about social history. I've got the six you asked for in the mini-bus. Can I leave them with

	you? I'm in a bit of a rush, I've got two more jobs to visit.

SPRATCHETT Get the guard to bring 'em over to the office.

MAGGIE Guard?

SPRATCHETT Yes, the warden, prison officer, screw? He'll bring them over, won't he?

MAGGIE Mr Spratchett, I don't think you quite understand. There is no guard. They're here on trust. I thought you'd had that explained to you.

SPRATCHETT What? No guard! Good God girl, what if they run amock? How are we to defend ourselves?

MAGGIE It is most unlikely that they'll run anywhere. They know the alternatives. If you have any problems you've got the superintendent's number on that sheet. We'll be dropping round from time to time.

SPRATCHETT From time to time! That's hardly adequate, Miss. I am quite sure the office did not agree . . .

MAGGIE Oh, one more thing.

SPRATCHETT Have you consulted the union over this one? Supervised prisoners is one thing, but . . .

MAGGIE They're not just boys. We try to run the home as close to normal social conditions as we can manage. There will be three girls in the group. Now please could you come and get them, I must be getting on. **(She walks off.)**

SPRATCHETT Girls! Look here, Miss, when I agreed to this scheme no one said anything about girls . . . I don't know who they think we are, up there in head office, expect us to stand guard over hooligans and muggers and girls, they're the worst, you know.

NIGEL They may not be muggers.

SPRATCHETT No, they may not. They may be molestets, or GBH merchants . . . just perfect for the municipal gardens wouldn't you say?

NIGEL   There are other crimes . . .

SPRATCHETT   That's as may be . . . We're not taking any chances. I'm going over to lock away the deck chairs and putting-course funds, and I want you to go and take all the chains off the men's toilets.

NIGEL   Do what?

SPRATCHETT   Take down the toilet chains. These vandals can wreak havoc with a toilet chain. And the paper too!

NIGEL   But what if people want to go to the toilet? What if they want to go to the toilet?

SPRATCHETT   If they want to go badly enough they'll find a way! *(Moves to leave.)*

NIGEL   I don't believe him.

SPRATCHETT   *(Over shoulder)* I should find a safe hiding-place for that pricker of yours. Find a cork! **(He walks off.)**

NIGEL   Find a cork? I don't believe it . . .

(Spratchett returns.)

SPRATCHETT   Those sluts wouldn't mess up the Ladies would they? I bet they would. Better get Molly to lock the Ladies up. **(He walks off.)**

NIGEL   But what if . . . No, I don't suppose you're worried. The man's a fully-fledged, paid-up nut-case.

(Enter REG, a gardener in his forties. Slow and considerate.)

REG   Who is?

NIGEL   Oh hello . . . that man Spratchett. There are times when he amazes me; that is, when he's not making me sick.

REG   Oh he's not that bad, all mouth most of the time. You know his wife died recently?

NIGEL   Not surprising!

REG   No, it was nasty, sudden, like one day she was there, next day she was gone. *(Pause)* And the terrible thing was, undertakers were on a work-to-rule. He had to have her lying round the house for a week.

NIGEL   Yeah, perhaps he's had his knocks, but that's no excuse for his technicolour nastiness.

REG   Hard on you, is he?

NIGEL   No, not on me. I humour him, usually . . . seems the best policy. No, it's his opinions, his way of looking at things, that gets me down.

REG   You're too sensitive. Let it wash over you like I do. Pays in the long run – you don't make enemies and you don't get ulcers.

NIGEL   Yes, I suppose you're right. Not that I make a fuss to his face. As I say, we get on all right. I suppose that's half the trouble. Guilt. I ought to confront him, make a stand. I let him get away with it.

REG   Can't see it myself. Best let it ride. You'll not change him by taking him head-on.

NIGEL   But he attacks everything head-on.

REG   It's the only way he knows.

NIGEL   But the way he talks about people . . . You should have heard him going on about this new lot of garden help.

REG   Who are they then?

NIGEL   Oh, there's a bunch from the new remand home. Didn't you know about them?

REG   I did hear talk of it. About time too. I'm weeks behind with the digging. I've got no tilth to speak of and we'll be planting out in a few days.

NIGEL   Does it worry you, working with criminals? Think you can manage?

REG   I have had no trouble in the past. Not many of them are what you'd call criminals. Not yet, anyway.

NIGEL   Well I'd better go and find a cork!

REG   Would you bring over a couple of forks and those two spades with new handles? They're in the corner of my shed. Don't want these kids hanging round – keep them busy if I can . . .

NIGEL   Yes, I'll bring them. I'm surprised Spratchett lets 'em use forks. **(He goes off.)**

REG   Almost too late with this digging, the frost can't get to that soil now, and fertilizer's hardly time to work, still better late than never.

(Enter ETHEL. **She is a tramp whose life is conducted through an imaginary set of relationships based on half-recalled memories and the rubbish she collects and carries with her in a portable shopping-trolley. She is searching.)**

ETHEL   Now where is it? I'm sure I've put it somewhere obvious. I'll try my desk again, it could have slipped down behind the *Reader's Digest* books. **(She rootles through the rubbish bin.)**

REG   Morning Ethel. How's things with you?

ETHEL   Ah yes, I was going to show you that letter from my son in Adelaide. Such a nice one this week, so full of news. **(She moves towards Reg. He knows the routine and goes on digging.)** Would you just hold on for a minute while I find it?

REG   Not just now Ethel, I'm busy.

ETHEL   Just for a moment, please. I won't be a moment. If you could just hold these papers, I could find the letter.

REG   *(Firm)* No! You can read me the letter when you find it.

ETHEL   *(Rummaging)* It's here somewhere. I won't be long, Enid, I'll have that bath after you, I'm just . . .

(Muttering, she begins to unload her trolley.)

(Spratchett marches on. He is behaving like an NCO in charge of a group of recruits and is not being deterred by the lack of any recognisable order in PETE, SIDNEY, CARLTON, DENISE, ARLENE, JO.**)**

SPRATCHETT   Keep to the path, step up now. No dawdling. You're on the firm's time now.

(Jo goes to investigate a plant.)

ON THE PATH! I said. Leave that alone, it's still alive, it doesn't need any help from you.

(The group sidle on. Sullen, oblivious. Dressed in shapeless but
newish overalls. Reg watches, leaning on a fork. Carlton is
talking to Arlene at the back.)

Come along there Sambo. We haven't got all day. Not
like where you come from. And you, young lady, you
should know better.

ARLENE   Are you going to take that Sambo shit?

CARLTON   It's nothing new, just genetic insecurity.

SPRATCHETT   I'm going to ignore that.

DENISE   You'll have to, won't you, 'cos you don't know what it
means.

(She has her overalls unbuttoned low in the front.)

SPRATCHETT   Now just button yourself up girl. I can see far too much.

DENISE   Like it, do you?

SPRATCHETT   Now don't arouse me, young lady.

DENISE   I'm not a miracle worker. Is this the garden then or does
this route march carry on for ever?

SPRATCHETT   This is it. Now get in line all of you.

(Pete has sat down on the bench and is rolling a fag.)

SPRATCHETT   'Ere you, GET UP. Smoking is forbidden, you heard the
warder. Smoking is not allowed on the job.

PETE   She's not a warder, she's a 'community care officer'. She
cares about our health. You don't. Want one?

SPRATCHETT   I'm just telling you to . . . NO! GET IN LINE!

(Pete slowly joins the group, which can in no way be described
as a line. This doesn't stop Spratchett behaving as if he's
addressing a squad.)

Now then, it'll come as no surprise to you . . . *(to Jo)*
Face this way! It'll come as no surprise to you that I do
not like having you in my park.

(Ethel, who has been lost in her own world of searching, emerges
with a battered hairbrush.)

ETHEL Ah, there it is! I must return it to the shop, they said it'd
be blue, it's got to be blue you see, she'll not have any
other, so it'll have to go back. Could you hold this please
while I find the receipt? . . . *(Some of this has coincided
with Spratchett's speech but now she has interrupted, to
his embarrassment.)*

SPRATCHETT Not now, Ethel.

ETHEL Just for a minute, really, I put it out ready . . .

SPRATCHETT I said NOT NOW.

*(He tries to put the hairbrush back into her hands, but is
somehow left with it.)* I don't want to help you,
WOMAN! Take the hairbrush, can't you see I'm busy?

ETHEL But you always say you're busy. You need a rest from that
beast of a District Officer, he's driving you too hard. Now
be a good boy and take this hairbrush back to . . .

SPRATCHETT GOD IN HEAVEN!

ETHEL Hush dear, not in front of the servants. *(In a
conspiratorial whisper)* They really oughtn't to see us
rowing like this. They'll get the wrong idea. Now all I ask
is for you to be reasonable and take . . .

JO I'll take the brush.

ETHEL Oh, how kind.

SPRATCHETT You mustn't pamper her. She's not all there you see.
We've tried to have her put away. Doesn't work, they say.
Should be in a loony bin. You see, I suppose the park's
cheaper.

JO She seems harmless enough.

SPRATCHETT Easy to say, young lady, easy to say. I call it
irresponsibility; she should be locked up.

**(Ethel starts to wheel her trolley across towards Spratchett. He
retreats. Nigel enters with tools.)**

ETHEL I'll have to see that man about the lift. I can't get her
wheelchair down those stairs.

SPRATCHETT Ah, thank God, Barrows. Get rid of her, take her over to
Molly.

NIGEL   *(Cheerful)* Come on, Ethel let's have you over here.

(Nigel leads Ethel out in search of Molly.)

PETE   You handled that very well!

CARLTON   Very enlightened!

SPRATCHETT   Enough out of you, Sambo. Now as I was saying, I don't like the idea of you lot in my park, not one bit. It goes against the grain, park's meant to be peaceful, a haven, not a lock-up, and if I had my way that's where you'd be – locked up. I don't approve of this community service nonsense – it's no punishment. You'll not learn your lesson that way, will you?

CARLTON   As I said, 'enlightened'.

SPRATCHETT   But since no one bothers to ask my opinion, I have to do what I'm told, something which comes naturally to me. So just remember, any rough stuff or any little excuse and it'll be back to the chokey for you, and that means you girls too.

REG   We weren't expecting girls, were we Mr Spratchett?

SPRATCHETT   No, we were not, Mr Jarvis. And I can tell you I don't think is is right. I intend to lodge a formal complaint. It's not fair . . . It puts you and me in a very unfortunate position.

DENISE   What position's that Mr . . . ?

SPRATCHETT   We're not equipped.

DENISE   Oh dear.

SPRATCHETT   It adds insult to injury and I'd be fully behind you, Mr Jarvis, if you refused to work with these young, these young . . . hussies!

REG   Oh no. I'm not bothered, as long as they'll work. Makes no odds to me.

SPRATCHETT   Well I'm certainly making an official complaint. Now you've had the rules explained by your ward . . . care officer. All you've got to remember is that you're here to work. Did you hear that, Mr Jarvis? Work. It's no picnic, not meant to be.

PETE   Now that's strange, I must have been misinformed.

SPRATCHETT   So, Mr Jarvis, they're all yours. I'll be in my office if there's any trouble. They're to have lunch from 12 to 1 p.m. and *(stage whisper)* keep an eye on the tools, you know, especially the forks.

REG   I'll do that, Mr Spratchett. Lunch at twelve.

SPRATCHETT   Right now, you'll do exactly what he says.

ARLENE   That'll make a change!

SPRATCHETT   I'm handing over. You know where to find me.

REG   We'll be all right Mr Spratchett.

(Spratchett leaves. Pete immediately settles down to roll a fag. Jo sits down on the grass, by the sign 'Do not walk on the Grass', cross-legged and vacant. Carlton tries to whisper something to Arlene, who shies away.)

REG   Don't mind him. Bark's worse than his bite, as they say.

DENISE   Well I thought he was rather sweet. Sexy really. You see I like older men.

REG   That's as may be *(unflustered)*. Has anyone ever done any gardening?

(No one answers.)

SID   *(Who up to now has stood still and absent)* I was in charge . . .

PETE   Not recently but I had this very desirable primary school teacher who'd let me water her plants if I was good, and I was, for a ten-year-old!

REG   *(To Sid)* What were you saying lad?

ARLENE   Yeah, mustard and cress it was at my school. On blotting paper, and if you were very clever you'd get an avocado pear stone of your very own. I never could get mine to sprout.

REG   What were you in charge of lad?

SID   Greenhouse at school.

REG   That sounds better than my school days.

SID   Wasn't bad. Broken glass used to get in the tomatoes though.

REG   Broken glass?

SID   They used to break the glass, by dropping knives from the home economics room. I spent most of the time cleaning up the glass.

REG   Why'd they do that?

SID   I don't know. We had to throw away the tomatoes. The courgettes were OK though, harder skin.

REG   Courgettes too. They're tricky.

SID   We grew green peppers too.

REG   Well we don't have to explain to you . . .

SID   Sid.

REG   Sid, how important it is to get a good tilth and that needs digging.

PETE   Shit!

REG   Yes, and that too, dig it in deep and it does the plants a power of good. Speaking of which there's four bags of horse manure from the police stables over by the gate. Why don't you and the coloured lad . . . what's your name by the way?

CARLTON   Carlton, and he's Pete.

REG   Well you and Pete bring those sacks over here.

PETE   Charmed!

REG   Sid, you and me'll start digging the big bed. Girls, you see the small bed, well that's been dug, but all over there's little weeds need to be picked out and burnt.

DENISE   Aw, ain't that a bit cruel, what they ever done to you?

REG   Nothing yet. But come spring each one of those'll be shooting up for all they're worth and the place'll be a mess.

ARLENE   My dad had weeds in his garden. Only a small patch mind you, but every Saturday he had me out there. Weeding and weeding.

REG   Oh good, so you have done some gardening.

ARLENE   Only enough to know that I hate it *(more venom than expected).*

DENISE   Are these the poor harmless little fellows?

REG   They're the ones. Put 'em on the path. We'll take them to the bonfire later.

(Sid has been cleaning a spade with great care – almost finickity.)

Now then Sid, never mind the dirt, it'll soon be dirty enough. Start up at this end here. Now the trick with digging is to take it steady and keep it orderly, a row at a time. Break up the soil, get the air to it. Then we'll put in the manure next time round. *(He remembers Jo and turns.)* And what about you then? *(Not expecting an answer.)*

JO   I've not had much experience, I'm afraid.

REG   Not to worry, know anything about bulbs?

JO   No, only pot plants.

REG   Ah, pot plants. They need careful looking after.

JO   Well, not once you've got them going.

REG   *(Puzzled)* That's true.

JO   It's the germination that's difficult, needs boiling water.

REG   Boiling water! What plant is that?

JO   Marijhuana. My boyfriend and I grow it.

REG   Ah, well that . . . that's not allowed is it?

JO   No, but the cops are so thick, they don't know the difference.

ARLENE   Not that thick, Jo.

JO   Yeah, that thick. That dope was just an excuse, we . . .

REG   Well I want you to plant these bulbs all round those trees. Take this trowel and dig a small hole and put them in with the point pointing upwards, all right?

JO   All right . . . can I walk in the grass to do it?

REG   Oh yes, just ignore the sign.

ARLENE   She will.

(**Enter Pete and Carlton making a lot of noise and fuss. They are dragging a bag of manure.**)

PETE   Phor . . . very fragrant this is.

CARLTON   Police horses you say.

REG   That's right.

CARLTON   Figures.

PETE   And where exactly would you like this dumped?

REG   Er, I'm not sure.

PETE   Oh now, don't tempt me.

CARLTON   Where to . . . sir . . . it is a little heavy.

REG   Put it on the path, next to Sid.

CARLTON   There you are Sidney, Z-Car shit – use it sparingly.

(**They dump it and some falls on Sid.**)

SID   Watch it, mind my trousers.

CARLTON   Mind his trousers, ducky. (**He lisps and camps it up but gets no response from Pete who goes off for the next lot. Carlton follows.**)

(**A man in a track suit, DONALD, rides in on a posh blue racing bike. Parks it. Puts a chain round the wheel and fork. Then looks at his watch, presses a button, it buzzes, he begins to jog past Denise and Arlene.**)

ARLENE   Aren't we going to see your legs then?

DONALD   'Fraid not darling. (*Forced fake cockney*) Must get a sweat up.

DENISE   I could help you do that.

DONALD	*(Distracted by her cleavage, trips.)* Oops, sorry, I mean no thanks . . . not now . . . anyway, sorry . . .
DENISE	Look where you're going.
DONALD	I will . . .
ARLENE	Those sort get right up my nose.
DENISE	Yes, but sexy in a sort of plummy, wholesome way.
	(Sid is working frantically.)
REG	Easy boy, easy. You'll not last the day like that.
SID	Got to get it done.
REG	All in good time.
SID	Don't want that keeper after me.
REG	Don't worry about him.
SID	He makes me nervous.
REG	Bark's worse than his bite.
SID	You said.
REG	Still at school are . . . were you?
SID	Just left.
REG	Like it?
SID	Not much.
REG	Why's that? *(Pause)* Bully you did they?
SID	A bit.
REG	You should try sticking up for yourself.
SID	What's the point? I just kept out of their way.
REG	Best policy.
SID	Wasn't that bad.
REG	What?
SID	Keeping out of the way. I had the greenhouse you see, and then Mr Painely . . .

(Carlton and Pete come on with another sack making even more fuss.)

PETE   That's the lot. I'll not do any more shit shifting. Why can't the girls do some? Sexual equality, that's your line isn't it? Fancy some of this do you? *(He takes some to Jo.)*

JO   *(Very cold)* Sod off!

PETE   Ooh sorry, what about you, fancy a little?

DENISE   Grow up!

CARLTON   Mr Spratshit . . . is that really his name?

REG   Spratchett.

CARLTON   Well, he said you shouldn't leave us unsupervised. I think he's afraid we might run off with all this invaluable organic matter.

REG   Put it over there. *(They move it.)*

PETE   Where's the toilet, governor?

REG   Past the pond, just by the tennis courts and as quick as you can.

PETE   I'm sure you'd be the first person to appreciate that you cannot hurry nature's way, ta ta!

CARLTON   And what should I do then?

REG   You can help the girls with the weeds, until I've finished this row, then you can take over from me.

(Carlton with some uncertainty goes and works as far from the girls as possible.)

REG   Who was this teacher then?

SID   Mr Painely.

REG   Good bloke was he?

SID   Good to me.

REG   How's that?

SID   Took an interest in my case.

REG   Case?

SID   Yeah . . . *(a little flustered)* yeah, me, my family, that sort of thing.

REG   Come round to your house, did he?

SID   Oh yeah, often.

REG   Why's that?

SID   Helping.

REG   Oh.

SID   He took me on trips. We went to Worthing, Brighton, Margate. We walked along the South Downs, youth hostels, all that.

REG   That sounds very . . . nice

DENISE   I went to Brighton on the back of this bloke's bike. Bank holiday. Dead sexy he was. You know, tight leathers and no sense on the by-pass.

ARLENE   Sounds hilarious.

DENISE   It didn't last though. He left me in Redhill when his camshaft went. I had to take the train.

CARLTON   Do you think that's a weed? *(It is a tentative attempt to make contact.)*

ARLENE   *(Moves away.)* They're all weeds, stupid, anything green. *(Pause.)*

CARLTON   Must be lunch-time soon?

ARLENE   I don't know. I've not got a watch. You have.

CARLTON   Oh yeah, oh no, only eleven. Can I help you with that bit?

ARLENE   S'all right, thank you. Shouldn't you be digging now? *(To Reg)* Shouldn't he, Mister?

REG   Shouldn't he what?

ARLENE   Be digging. Carlton, you said you had to go off somewhere.

REG   That's right . . . I almost forgot. Here take my spade, it's balanced.

CARLTON   *(To Arlene)* Thank you.

REG   Now keep it tidy. Sid'll show you how, won't you Sid?

SID   Sure, you've got to dig deep. I use my foot.

CARLTON   I know how to dig you silly poof!

REG   None of that, lad. We'll have none of that.

CARLTON   Sorry – just tell him I'm not a 'thick black' will you?

SID   I never said you were.

DENISE   Boys . . . temper, temper.

(Reg goes off.)

SID   I never said . . .

CARLTON   All right, all right, I'm sorry, just forget it. Let's dig.

(They dig. Carlton vents his annoyance at Arlene's rebuff on the earth. Enter three lads. Two in school uniform, one not. BRIAN, KEVIN and LEN. They are scruffy fifth-years.)

KEVIN   He'll not catch us. Sit down.

LEN   Last time he said he'd get the welfare onto my mum.

KEVIN   Look, he's not got the time, relax, look at me.

BRIAN   Yeah, look at you. Not a pretty sight.

KEVIN   Not beautiful, but cool. No worries, see?

BRIAN   My dad'd carve me up if he knew about this.

KEVIN   No, the point is, Higgins may talk big when he's got you in his office, but he's overworked . . . Think of all the skivers he's got in his year. He can never keep up with 'em.

BRIAN   But he uses a helicopter.

KEVIN   A what?

BRIAN   He's got a friend who's got a helicopter, he told us.

KEVIN   You're joking!

LEN   No, I heard it too. Patrols the park. I've heard it.

KEVIN   What a bunch of wallies!

BRIAN   Well how else did he know we was hopping maths, and where we went?

LEN   And when we went there?

KEVIN   I don't know, but he certainly does not have a friend with a helicopter. Oh my gawd, you two. Those are police helicopters, you jerks. He must think you are a right bunch of pussy willows.

BRIAN   Well Morgan believed it.

LEN   And those crafty sods from 5KL.

KEVIN   Well that only confirms what I already knew, that if you are thick enough to hang around school, you will believe anything. Hey up. It's Mary Peters.

(They see Donald, who is jogging round the park. They cheer and follow him off.)

DENISE   Noisy little bastards. They should be in school.

ARLENE   I don't blame them. I wish I'd hopped it more often.

DENISE   Well I did, and now I regret it. Can't get a job with no qualifications.

ARLENE   You can't get a job because you're a woman. Good for one thing only.

DENISE   Well I'm quite good at that.

ARLENE   See what I mean?

(The lads return. Kevin has seen the bike. They circle it, making admiring noises. At a signal from Kevin, they pick up the bike bodily and trot off into the trees.)

DENISE   Cheeky.

ARLENE   They'll not get away with it.

CARLTON   'Course they will.

ARLENE   Someone nicked my bike from right outside our house, and it's not that sort of area.

CARLTON   That's the sort of area they work in. You've got to make it secure *(Sensing an opening)* I could show you how to make it secure . . . if you wanted.

ARLENE   *(Coldly)* I don't have a bike now, do I?

CARLTON   No . . . I don't suppose you do.

DENISE   Where you live then? Posh is it?

ARLENE   We only moved last year, Barnet. Used to live round here. I went to school near here, but then we got this house. Been my dad's ambition to move out, saved and saved.

DENISE   What's he do then, your dad?

ARLENE   Works for the council. Building surveyor. He stops people getting decent houses.

CARLTON   How's that, crooked is he?

ARLENE   No. The opposite. He checks that they're all up to standard, see . . . He's got a book, called the Parker Morris Standard. In there it tells you everything about how a house should be. Windows, doors, ceilings, everything. He's got a million excuses why a house isn't up to standard. And he uses them.

DENISE   What, to stop people living in 'em?

ARLENE   Precisely!

JO   But why? Are they dangerous?

ARLENE   'Course not. It's tiny things mostly. Window a centimetre too small, doors an inch too far over. Drives the builders mad so they just give up. Do you know those new brick houses down Brighton Way?

DENISE   Nice.

ARLENE   Empty.

DENISE   What! All of them?

ARLENE   All of them. Every single one has got something wrong. Now the builders have gone off to another job. But 'cos of my dad no one can live there.

JO   But why?

ARLENE   'Preserve standards.' According to my dad, standards have
             got to be maintained, whatever the cost. He says no one
             cares about standards and that's why the country's in a
             mess.

DENISE   Doesn't make sense to me. My auntie's got five kids and
             she's been waiting for years for a flat, she's living . . .

ARLENE   That's why I did it.

DENISE   Did it?

ARLENE   Set fire to it.

CARLTON   Set fire to what?

ARLENE   His garage.

DENISE   You set fire to his garage?

ARLENE   He'd built it himself. All to the Parker Morris Standards.
             Shelves, racks, cupboards, louvered doors, fitted plugs,
             the lot.

DENISE   And you burnt it!

ARLENE   Started it with paraffin.

JO   That was pretty destructive.

ARLENE   It was the only thing he understood, you see.

CARLTON   But what did he do?

ARLENE   What do you think? That's why I'm here.

JO   Couldn't you have explained?

ARLENE   You try explaining to a rule book.

CARLTON   That is pretty bloody amazing.

DENISE   And he turned you in?

ARLENE   Had to, otherwise he'd not get the insurance. Anyway,
             my clothes stunk of paraffin. *(Pause.)*

MRS WALTON   *(Off)* Selwyn, Selwyn, SELWYN. **(She enters in an
             agitated state.)** Lord God where is that boy? When I catch
             'im I goin' to get his daddy to give 'im licks that put 'im
             outta circulation for a week. He headstrong that boy. I
             can't put up with 'im much longer now. Mister *(to*

Carlton). Hey, Mister Gardener, Sir. Have you seen a young black boy hanging round the park?

CARLTON No, I ain't the gardener and I ain't seen no boy. Shouldn't he be in school?

MRS WALTON 'Course he should. Of course he should. But I getta call from the school sayin' he not in, and where is he, and is he sick? I'm so ashamed to have to tell 'em I don't know.

CARLTON No need to be ashamed. Boys will be boys.

MRS WALTON But my daughter, she was a perfect pupil. Me and her daddy so proud of her and now this Selwyn boy goin' to let us down bad. Truantin' just the beginning. Too many of these black boys gettin' into trouble these days an I don' want my Selwyn mixin' with all them Rasta yout' or whatever.

CARLTON There's no harm in that. He's lookin' for his identity, his history.

MRS WALTON Back home is his history an' there he wouldn't have got away with nothin'. Him granny gotta strap an' she use it. Him soon learn right from wrong.

CARLTON But that's not goin' to work here, now is it?

MRS WALTON I don' see why not. Discipline still discipline wherever you is. St Lucia, Kensal Rise or Timbuctoo. An' if I lays my hans on that boy, that's where he gonna wish he was, Timbuctoo. There's a policeman, maybe he can help. Maybe he seen him.

CARLTON Oh no missus, don't ask him, he'll just . . . How can she be so stupid? She gonna lose that boy.

DENISE 'Fraid so.

(As Mrs Walton goes off she meets SONIA, **her daughter, who is returning from college.)**

MRS WALTON Sonia, thank God. I found you at last. Have you seen Selwyn anywhere? I've been looking everywhere.

SONIA 'Course not, Mum. I've only just arrived. He's in school, isn't he?

MRS WALTON   That's just the trouble. He ain't. They rung me up and want to know where he is. I told them I thought he was at school and . . .

SONIA   Oh no, not that again.

MRS WALTON   Well I tell them. They the ones who should know where he is. He's their responsibility during the day. How can I tell where he is . . .

SONIA   Don't be foolish Mum. If he bunks off, that's his business. You can't blame them. What can they do if he's not there? They only ring you up to check and let you know.

MRS WALTON   Well sometimes I think I'd rather not know. How come it never happened with you?

SONIA   You can't spend your time comparin' him to me. We're different. I wanted to be there. You can't force anyone to stay there if they don't want to.

MRS WALTON   Somebody goin' to have to force him, because I am certainly not goin' to run aroun' after him like this for much longer. And then his father goin' to get back at me for not controllin' him.

SONIA   Does he have to know?

MRS WALTON   Of course he has to know . . . well maybe not . . . if I find him quick and take him back. Will you go an' check back at the house?

SONIA   Sorry Mum. I'm here to meet Doreen. She's just had this interview for a job and I said I'd meet her here. Anyway I've got to get back to college by twelve.

MRS WALTON   Yes, yes, I understand. I don' want that Selwyn to be distractin' you from your study. He ain't that important.

SONIA   Well it's not that . . .

MRS WALTON	I'll try that policeman. Maybe he will help me. I'll see you this evenin'.
SONIA	See you . . . Good luck!
	(DOREEN **has come up behind her. She is dressed as for an interview.**)
DOREEN	Who needs luck when you got talent and charm and brains and . . .
SONIA	Don't tell me, gal . . .
DOREEN	All right, I won't then.
SONIA	You got it?
DOREEN	They made me an offer an I'm considerin' it. Considerin' their terms of employment.
SONIA	Don't act so foolish, you mean to tell me you didn't accept it when they offered it?
DOREEN	Oh of course I accepted it. *(Her initial showy exuberance has disappeared.)* If I considered their terms of employment I'd never have walked into the place. I tell you it's exploitation. Slavery days all over again.
SONIA	Oh come on na. It ain't that bad. It's regular money at least. A bit of independence.
DOREEN	True. But God, Sonia, it's so borin'. I ain't even started and I bored just thinkin' about it. Tap, tap, tap . . . ooh shit . . . sorry ma'am . . . tap, tap, tap.
SONIA	It's a start. It took you long enough to get it.
DOREEN	Could be the finish. You know I was so damn excited when they tell me that I got the job. Just gettin' it seemed so cool. Then I remembered that I'd just had the best bit. You know I began to wish I'd gone to college like you.
SONIA	College ain't exactly so fantastic.
DOREEN	I know, I know . . . and anyway I don't want to talk about it. Let's go to the cafe and spend some o' this money which I am supposed to be makin' . . .
	(**They go off.**)
ARLENE	And what about you?
DENISE	Oh, my mum was all right. Anyway too busy to care most of the time.

ARLENE   So, how'd you get done?

DENISE   Oh, came natural to me. In the family you see . . . I'd been done before. Nicking mostly. Woolworths, kids' stuff.

ARLENE   So what got you on this caper?

DENISE   Oh a bunch of us had a racket going down West. Peter Robinson. Selfridges. Small stuff mostly, blouses, scarves, knickers, bras. Fun mostly, nothing much in it for us. Then I was picked up by this plain clothes copper in the changing room. I was stuffing this silk nightie down me tights.

CARLTON   What? A bloke?

DENISE   Don't be stupid. I think a bloke might have looked a little conspicuous in the ladies' changing room at Selfridges.

CARLTON   A woman cop!

ARLENE   They do have 'em you know.

DENISE   'Course I tried to run, but the bitch got me in the main doorway. Right embarrassing. Had me up against the escalator and then complained 'cos I wouldn't keep still. Hit me. *(Pause)* Bitch.

CARLTON   They're all the same. One time when I was up the Junction, me and my friend was just . . .

(The girls are not listening. Carlton's story is interrupted by Donald who has returned to find his bicycle gone.)

DONALD   Bloody hell . . . some little bastards . . . Did you see them? Someone's nicked my bike! Christ, I'll get them.

(He goes off, outraged.)

CARLTON   Who me bass . . . I didn't see nothin, masa, me just a dumb nigga. Ain't seen no man, no place, no how . . .

(The girls have a quick chuckle about the bike, but don't seem to notice Carlton's show. An ice-cream van chimes in the distance.)

DENISE   I'm fed up with this weedin'. I'm off to get a choc-ice.

CARLTON	Could you get me one? You want one, Arlene?
ARLENE	No thanks.
CARLTON	I'll pay. *(He is ignored.)*
DENISE	Are you sure? I'll stand you.
ARLENE	Oh, well, thanks Denise, I'll have a Mivvi.

(Sounds of dub on a cheap tape recorder. **Enter three West Indians – Rasta hats, moving to the music: WENDELL, NORRIS and SYLVAN. They are out of work. They are not talking, but each is taking a different bass line and giving his version. The tape runs out.)**

WENDELL	Dread guy.
NORRIS	You should hear the latest on Fat Man Hi Fi.
SYLVAN	Fat Man soun' playin' down Phoebe's tonight?
NORRIS	Junior tell me, but he can't take his bass 'cos he meeting some auntie from Guyana.
SYLVAN	Junior did meke that box in woodwork, in school.
NORRIS	Nicked the speaker from the assembly hall. Woodwork teacher think he mekin' a dresser for his mom.
WENDELL	I thought Junior been suspended from the sixth form.
NORRIS	Tha's right, he had a few friends into the common room, hear some soun's and these boys light up.
WENDELL	Ganga.
NORRIS	Sure ting.
WENDELL	Wowee guy.
SYLVAN	I thought I saw Junior down the labour las' Monday. Causin' a rumpus 'cos they wan' to give 'im a pressin' job down Shacklewell.
NORRIS	Junior always talkin' about the print.
SYLVAN	Big money in print. Kingsley makin' seventy poun' a week.
NORRIS	Sez Kingsley.

WENDELL Kingsley gotta car, guy.

NORRIS Not for long, way Kingsley drive it.

WENDELL You hear this. Prince Jah and the Righteous.

(*A new tape is switched on. The boys move on picking out their own version to it. They see Carlton.*)

NORRIS Hold on a minute. Ain't that Carlton Silsby? Heh Carlton, how you doin' man?

CARLTON (*Slips into a kind of dialect we haven't heard before.*) Me not bad, how you mekin'?

NORRIS But Carlton, why you workin'?

CARLTON Sort of.

WENDELL No money in gardenin', Carlton.

SYLVAN Tha's a fine suit they give you Carlton. Sexy mover.

CARLTON Burton's to rarse. No, ain't exactly for money.

NORRIS What you mean, NO MONEY? Man you hard up or sumptin'?

CARLTON Probation, in' it? Community service. Them ketch me rarse.

NORRIS Community service. That soun' fine Carlton.

WENDELL How long for?

CARLTON One blad clat year.

SYLVAN Soun' better than remand home. My brother just come back from Latchmere House. Tough guy. Before you go in this filth feel up your arse 'ole.

WENDELL Why he do that?

SYLVAN Lookin' for a file or sumptin'.

WENDELL A file?

SYLVAN An' any damn thing you do, bam – solitary and dey beat you guy.

NORRIS Babylon!

(**At this point Donald returns with a** PC **and** WPC.)

DONALD	That's where it was officer. Chained up. Right against that tree.
PC	Chained to the tree?
DONALD	Well no, actually, chained to itself.
PC	Nowadays you should chain it to something.
DONALD	Well it's never happened here before.

(He stares at Jo, Carlton, Arlene and the black boys.)

WPC	*(To Jo)* Did you see anything, dear?
JO	No.
WPC	Nothing at all?
JO	I said NO.

(The black lads are trying to sidle out.)

PC	Just a minute, you lot.
NORRIS	You hear sumptin' boy?
PC	I said, wait a minute.
WENDELL	We're jus' passin' through guy.
PC	Well just pass back this way.
NORRIS	Not again!
WPC	What about you love? You see anything?
ARLENE	Well there was . . .
CARLTON	Nothing. We've seen not anything. *(Astounded that Arlene should give anything away.)*
WPC	Go on love.
ARLENE	Well there was this person pushing . . .
WPC	A bike?
ARLENE	No more a shopping basket on wheels.
CARLTON	Oh yeah, you're right. She was a bit suspicious.
WPC	What did she look like?

ARLENE   Well, she was about . . . this tall. And she had on these yellow rubber boots . . .

CARLTON   No, no, she was . . . this tall and they weren't rubber boots, they was cowboy boots with spurs and . . .

(**During this conversation the PC has been routinely questioning the boys. One of them has sworn.**)

PC   All right, that's the way you want it. Turn around. Hands against the tree. *(To WPC)* Can you call for a car? *(She goes off.)*

NORRIS   But man, we done nothin'.

PC   Shut up and hands on the tree.

(**He pushes them roughly against the tree. He spots Wendell's tape recorder.**)

Where'd this come from?

WENDELL   It's mine, guy.

PC   Where'd you nick it 'guy'?

WENDELL   I bought it.

PC   You working?

WENDELL   I was.

PC   Sounds likely. And what about you?

NORRIS   *(Muttering)* Kiss me rarse!

PC   Charming. Is this the way they teach you to talk back home?

NORRIS   This is my home.

PC   Don't push your luck sonny.

(Police siren in the distance. WPC returns.)

WPC   They're on their way.

PC   Right you lot, let's move it. Take this, 'possible receiving'.

NORRIS   But what we done guy?

PC   Suspicion. Now shut up and move.

CARLTON   But they done . . .

PC	And you keep yourself buttoned up, sunshine.
ARLENE	Christ, but they were just walking through the park.

(They are about to move when Spratchett runs up.)

SPRATCHETT	Trouble, officer?
PC	Stolen bike. Taking these three in on suspicion.
SPRATCHETT	Quite right. I've had trouble from these coloureds before.
NORRIS	But we've never been here before.
SPRATCHETT	Well they're all the same. If you need any help, officer, I can lend a . . .
PC	No thanks. Come on, move . . .
SPRATCHETT	We'll teach them a lesson, eh gal?
WPC	I think you can leave us now. We'll manage.
SPRATCHETT	Oh no, I'll see you to the gate. Wouldn't miss this for the world.

(All go off, Carlton and Arlene follow, shouting abuse. They are brought together. Donald and Jo are left.)

DONALD	God, I hope it was them.
JO	It wasn't.
DONALD	How do you know?
JO	Because I saw who did nick your fancy bloody bike.
DONALD	Well why didn't you say?
JO	What and help the pigs?
DONALD	It would get those black lads off.
JO	It wouldn't have got them off. It's only suspicion remember.
DONALD	Suspicion of stealing my bike.
JO	That's what you think.

DONALD   Oh I don't know . . . all I know is that bike cost me a hundred-and-fifty quid.

JO   Wow!

(Donald goes off. Jo goes back to planting bulbs. Sid continues to dig. Enter the Man in the Black Coat. He stands and stares at Sid.)

MAN   Working hard are you?

SID   Got to be done.

MAN   That's true.

(Pete walks over from the opposite side.)

PETE   *(To Jo)* Where's Denise?

JO   Went to get an ice cream.

PETE   Oh, I could do with one of those. Which side'd she go?

(Pete walks past Man in the Black Coat, who recognises him. Man is stunned. He starts to follow. Thinks better of it. He turns on Sid.)

MAN   What the hell are you doing here anyway?

SID   Digging. Like I said. *(Surprised at vehemence.)*

MAN   But why you . . . why him?

SID   Oh, community service. From the centre down Church Street.

MAN   Punishment, is it?

SID   Sort of.

MAN   *(Viciously)* Hardly. (He goes off in the opposite direction.)

(Pete and Denise come back, eating ice lollies.)

PETE   Bloody marvellous 'en it!

DENISE   Don't surprise me.

PETE   No bloody paper and no bloody chains.

DENISE   Deliberate, you reckon?

PETE   'Course it is.

DENISE Ladies was locked.

PETE It's that bastard park keeper, filthy he is.

DENISE He has got a way with him.

PETE You know, Denise, this ice lolly reminds me of something, I can't quite put my finger on it . . . can you . . .

DENISE Oh piss off.

(Nigel comes on.)

NIGEL Have you seen Mr Spratchett?

PETE You mean that jumped up Nazi squadie?

NIGEL Mr Spratchett. Park keeper. My boss.

PETE Poor sod.

NIGEL Have you seen him?

PETE No, and long may it last. Did he take the chains off the toilets?

NIGEL Er, well yes, he did.

PETE For Chrissake, why?

NIGEL Vandals. He is a very careful man.

PETE Don't give me that. He's a nutter.

NIGEL Frightened.

PETE He's a bastard.

DENISE He's your boss?

NIGEL He's a frightened bastard and he's my boss.

DENISE Give you a hard time, does he?

NIGEL Sometimes, but I get round him.

PETE Can't see how you stand it. If he was my boss I'd kick him in the . . .

DENISE Don't be soft. You've not got the guts.

NIGEL Put up with his ways. He could make life pretty rough for me. You have to get along, don't you?

JO   No, you don't.

         (**Carlton and Arlene come back. They are outraged.**)

CARLTON That's marvellous 'en it?

ARLENE   They'll do anything to clobber your lot.

CARLTON Believe me, that was nothing.

DENISE   What was nothing?

ARLENE   Police took away some of Carlton's friends.

CARLTON On suspicion.

PETE   Of what?

ARLENE   Of nicking that track-suited burk's bike.

DENISE   But it was that scruffy lot from school.

CARLTON 'Course it was, but that doesn't matter.

ARLENE   And that Spratchett. He's a nasty piece of work. You
         should have heard what he was saying about the
         coloured . . .

CARLTON Blacks.

ARLENE   About the blacks. Shockin'.

CARLTON He should be put away. He's earning taxpayers' money,
         that racist git. Race Relations Act, my arse.

JO   *(To Nigel)* And you put up with that too, do you?

NIGEL   I don't hear it too often.

CARLTON Well you wouldn't, would you?

JO   So you let him get away with it, do you?

NIGEL   Best policy.

JO   For you maybe. Perhaps you're a racist too.

NIGEL   Don't be daft, 'course I'm not.

JO   Well then you sodding well ought to do something about
         it, say something.

NIGEL   Well I do . . . I will.

JO Ha! Some hope. You're all the same you liberals. Got big opinions, but you don't let 'em get in the way of your precious job, your hi fi and payments on the MGB.

NIGEL I've not got an MGB.

JO I'm off to lunch, before I throw up.

DENISE Good idea. Coming Arlene?

PETE Yeah.

DENISE Not you, I said 'Arlene'.

(**They all go off to lunch.**)

CARLTON Come on then. Got to keep trying. You coming Sidney?

PETE Naw, not 'im *(uncertain)*.

CARLTON Why not, good for a laugh!

PETE No, let's leave him alone.

SID I'll just finish this row.

CARLTON *(Lisping)* You do that Sidney, my love. He's funny that one. Queer I should say, pansy eh?

PETE Could be. *(He is not joining the banter as they go off.)*

(**Nigel tidies tools. Sid digs. Enter Susie with her packed lunch. Sits on the bench. Nigel sees her. Indecision. Tidies half-heartedly. Sees a bag of manure by bench. Moves over.**)

NIGEL I'll just move this manure. Must put you off.

SUSIE No, don't worry.

NIGEL I'll move it.

SUSIE All right.

(**Nigel moves it. More indecision. He makes a decision and goes to sit on the bench. He loses his nerve.**)

NIGEL Not a bad day for March.

SUSIE My first day in the park, for lunch, that is.

NIGEL Thought I hadn't seen you before.

SUSIE   No.

NIGEL   'Course I saw you this morning . . . *(weak laugh)*. Silly really.

SUSIE   Nice, though.

NIGEL   Got to keep my spirits up.

SUSIE   I suppose so.

(Pause.)

NIGEL   Do you work near here?

SUSIE   For the council. Social services.

NIGEL   Sounds interesting.

SUSIE   Can be.

(Pause: Nigel summons up his courage.)

NIGEL   Perhaps, I could . . . we . . . I mean . . .

(Spratchett comes across, shouting.)

SPRATCHETT   BARROWS! What are you doing boy? Those hooligans are having their lunch in the children's play area.

NIGEL   *(Attempting cool)* So what?

SPRATCHETT   Well do something about it. Clear 'em out before someone gets hurt.

NIGEL   But they're not harming anyone.

SPRATCHETT   Don't argue with me lad. Just hurry up and do it.

NIGEL   All right! Perhaps I'll see you again?

(He runs off.)

SUSIE   Perhaps.

(Sid finishes digging. Rakes it over carefully.)

SUSIE   That's a very tidy job.

SID   It'll do.

(Sid goes off for his lunch. Susie continues to eat her lunch.)

SCENE 2   **The same. It is night.**
      (Enter DOREEN **and** SONIA. **They have been to the club.)**

DOREEN   What's the matter Sonia?

SONIA   Nothin' that concerns you.

DOREEN   Come on gal, don' act feisty with me. I'm your friend, remember? Is it Sylvan?

SONIA   Don' talk to me 'bout that . . .

DOREEN   What you fall out with 'im?

SONIA   Kind of. We ain't talkin' cause of a little disagreement.

DOREEN   What are goin' to disagree about with a lovely lookin' black boy like Sylvan?

SONIA   Oh yeah, he's good lookin'. I'm not denyin' that, but . . .

DOREEN   But what? It was a good party. It's not 'cause he in trouble with . . .

SONIA   It's nothin' to do with that. The pigs pick up anyone on sus, these days.

DOREEN   As long as they is black.

SONIA   Yeah. I ain't goin' to hold that against 'im.

DOREEN   Well come on na gal. What's the problem? Is it sex? He bin pushin' you too far? If he's a friend of Norris that wouldn't surprise me, that boy just never stops.

SONIA   No. No. Jus' wish he was. That seems like the furthest thing from his mind. Naw, it's his music, music, music: King Tubby, Big Yout, Jah Stitch, Always dub. We never get to go to the pictures or to the disco. Always the clubs and sounds and Skank.

DOREEN	But you liked it.
SONIA	Yeah, I still do in moderation, but I like soul and disco souns too. Try tellin' that to Sylvan.
DOREEN	Have you tried compromise?
SONIA	There's no compromise with the disciples of Jah, didn't you know? They's always on the search for righteousness . . . huh.

(SYLVAN **comes on. He is quoting.**)

SYLVAN	All across the nation
	Black man suffers aggravation
	Babylon them rule de streets
	Black boys fight an' pigs retreats.
	Peace and tranquillity be with you . . . and where the hell you get to lady?
SONIA	*(Impressed)* Sylvan, you make that up?
SYLVAN	Sure ting guy.
DOREEN	He got it from a book.
SYLVAN	Shut yo' mouth.
DOREEN	You gonna mek me? You got it from that book your brother bring home from school.
SYLVAN	I done adapted it, so shut yo' face before I . . .
SONIA	Heh, heh, heh you two. Take it easy.
SYLVAN	All right sista, you tell that to my woman, she feisty for no reason an' I ain't takin' it no more.

(NORRIS **and** WENDELL **follow. They are stoned and making their own music.**)

NORRIS	Dread souns.

(He settles down to cuddle with Doreen.)

WENDELL	Revolution is the only solution.
	So Jah say to the righteou' brederin'.

(He does a little dance to his own bass beat.)

SYLVAN	Babylon can't pin nothin' on us guy.

NORRIS   Don' you be so sure. Justice is a white ting in dis country.

WENDELL   Savin' the people from utter damnation.
Jah knows the ways of his people's desperation.
Roots, rules and black tribulation.

SYLVAN   Don' walk in the street at night. Black boys ain't safe des days.

NORRIS   Too true, too true.

SYLVAN   Come na sister. You look sexy when you angry.

    (Wendell is gyrating until he comes across ETHEL **who has wandeѕed on during the last few lines.)**

WENDELL   Salutations sister.

ETHEL   Ah, there you are, at last.

WENDELL   You talkin' to me?

ETHEL   There's so much packing to do. I can't leave until it's all done.

WENDELL   What a pity. White lady can't leave 'til she done her packin'. *(He has turned belligerent.)* We ain't Kunte Kinte lady. We stiksmen.

NORRIS   *(Interrupting in a friendly tone)* Don' worry, we'll help.

ETHEL   I know it's a nuisance but . . .

DOREEN   Yeah, we'll help you pack. Is there much more to do?

ETHEL   Oh how kind of you. I'm all at sixes and sevens. I don't know where I am.

SYLVAN   An' this here is your suitcase, is it? We'll get it packed now, won't we Wendell?

SONIA   Come on, we don't want you to be late.

    (Helps Ethel with her coat.)

WENDELL   Aw come on. Les leave her. Huh!

ETHEL   Well that's most awfully kind. You see I'm meant to be going by train.

NORRIS   Don' worry, we'll catch your train.

SYLVAN   Almost ready.

DOREEN   Where you goin' in such a hurry?

ETHEL   To my cousin in Dunstable. It's her anniversary, you see.

DOREEN   Well give her our regards.

ETHEL   I'll do that. How kind. Now we're almost ready. Would you boys be kind enough to walk me to the station.

NORRIS   Be a pleasure. Eh Wendell?

WENDELL   Maybe.

SYLVAN   A real privilege.

ETHEL   But my hat . . . I can't go without my hat.

           (Wendell has picked up the hat and has put it on top of his own. Sonia sees it and rescues it from the gyrating figure.)

SONIA   Is this it?

ETHEL   Ah yes, there it is. Now I hope I've got everything.

           (They form a procession. Wendell still chanting at the front. Norris takes Ethel by the arm. Sonia takes the other. Sylvan wheels the basket, with Sonia on his arm.)

           So nice to have three big strong gentlemen to protect me.

DOREEN   Don' forget the women sister. We is the real protectors aroun' here.

ETHEL   You never know these days, do you? The streets just aren't safe any more. More's the pity.

NORRIS   You can say that again, lady.

WENDELL   Babylon is threatenin' . . . heh
           White man is frightenin'
           Black man is sufferin'.

           (They all parade off.)

                              End of Act One

ACT TWO

SCENE 1   Two months later. It's May. The bulbs are out and there are
wallflowers in the beds. There is a summery feel – the young
offenders are more settled. They have personalised their clothing.
Bird song. THE MAN IN THE BLACK COAT is sitting on the
bench, waiting.

(SID comes on, confident in his role as gardener. These are his
plants. He is staking them up and deadheading. He is talking to
himself and the plants. NIGEL is picking up litter. He greets Sid.
MRS WALTON walks across. She is dressed up to go out. She has
been crying.)

NIGEL   Morning, Mrs Walton. Still looking for Selwyn?
(Cheerfully until he sees her face) Oh dear, what's up?
Are you all right?

MRS WALTON   Quite all right, thank you.

NIGEL   You don't look it. Here, sit down a minute. *(She
hesitates.)* Come on. Sit down for a minute. Is it Selwyn?
(She nods. Then sits. She begins to sniff.) What's up?
Trouble at school? *(She shakes her head.)* Can't be that
bad.

MRS WALTON   It is, Mr Park Keeper, sir, it is.

NIGEL   Come on. What's up? *(She needs persuading.)* Where are
you off to?

MRS WALTON   I gotta go down the police station. They got 'im down
there.

NIGEL   Oh dear, that's not very good, is it?

MRS WALTON   It's never happened in our family. The very first time.
The shame of it.

NIGEL   Oh, it's not that bad, though.

MRS WALTON   And what's his daddy goin' to say? He gonna kill 'im. So help 'im God, he'll kill him.

NIGEL   What's he supposed to have done?

MRS WALTON   They didn't say. Just that they got 'im and I gotta go down an answer for 'im. Oh Lard, how am I goin' to break this to his daddy, I jus' don't know.

NIGEL   I'm sure he'll understand. Won't be as bad as you think. It's probably not serious.

MRS WALTON   It's those friends of his. Those boys from the youth club. They gone lead 'im astray, just as I predicted. All their Rastaman rubbish, it ain't right for a boy of his age to be mixin' with that sort. I can't stop 'im, he don't listen to me or his daddy . . .

NIGEL   Well I suggest you get on down to the police station. I'm sure it won't be as terrible as you think. Probably just routine enquiries.

MRS WALTON   Whatever it is, it's a shameful thing for a mother to have to pick up her son from the policemen. No one ever been caught by the police in our family. I don' understand it, I really don't.

(She wanders off.)

NIGEL   Good luck.

(Nigel continues to pick up litter. Sid talks to him.)

SID   This'll need hoeing again soon. Can't let it get out of hand. Come on my little beauty, you need a little support, else the wind'll have you.

(JO joins them. She has an air of one who has mastered inactivity. She sits on the grass and smokes.)

JO   What you doing?

SID   Deadheading.

JO   What's that?

SID   Taking off the dead flowers so that others grow.

JO   I think the dead bloom's romantic.

SID   Stops them growing. Nothing romantic in that.

JO   You like gardening, don't you?

SID   Suppose so.

JO   Suits you.

SID   Perhaps.

JO   What'll you do after?

SID   Hoeing's next and then mulch.

JO   No, when we've finished this business, what then?

SID   Keeps the moisture in.

JO   Will you go back to your family?

SID   The sun'll get to their roots.

JO   You have got a family?

SID   And then it's the liquid manure. Nurture them.

JO   You're being very evasive.

SID   Plants don't ask questions.

JO   I don't mean to be nosey . . . I don't even know what you're in for. Do you know what I was done for?

SID   No.

JO   Would you like to know?

SID   Don't mind.

JO   It wasn't for dope. That was just their excuse.

SID   Would you pass me those stakes please?

JO   We were having it off.

SID   No, the small ones.

JO   In the back of his Morris Traveller. You'd be amazed at the room, and it had curtains. Flowered ones. He was an art teacher you see. He lived in this Morris 1000 Traveller. Not all the time. He had a wife and kids somewhere.

SID   They've got a wooden frame, haven't they?

JO   Plenty of room in the back for all sorts of things.

SID   They don't make 'em any more you know.

JO   It was after this staff party. I shouldn't have been there, dead secret. He'd have been sacked if they'd known. It's not allowed with students you see.

SID   This soil's too dry already.

JO   We were having a right old time in the back, when these coppers look in. Knock on the door, barge in. Well they like it, you see. 'Course we weren't breaking the law, so they searched the van, found some grass and that was it. He'd been had up before and I got done with him. Pigs. They just liked to have an excuse. We weren't even naked. I mean, not totally.

SID   Pass me that hoe.

JO   You're very strange, you know.

SID   Could be.

JO   Do you like girls or boys?

SID   Don't mind.

JO   Don't mind?

SID   Not interested, either way.

JO   Are you gay?

SID   Gay?

JO   Homosexual. Do you like other boys instead of girls?

SID   Not given it much thought.

JO   I think you are. I've got lots of gay friends. I like them, sort of understanding. 'Course the pigs hate them. Threatens their piggy manhood, I suppose.

SID   What'll you do after?

JO   Don't know. Just drift, I suppose. Something'll come up, it usually does. I want a bit of freedom, make my own decisions, don't want them to push me around. I've had enough of that. What about you?

SID   More of the same I expect.

JO   You'll miss the gardens, won't you?

SID   'Spect so.

(DONALD **rides in on his bike, a new one. He has a chain and carefully chains it to the park bench. He jogs off.**)

DONALD   Bed's coming along nicely.

SID   Thanks.

JO   Aren't you ever going to take those trousers off?

DONALD   'Fraid not.

(**Jo returns to her seat and begins to doodle on the 'Do Not Walk on the Grass' sign. Enter** CARLTON **and** ARLENE. **They have been trapped by** ETHEL. **Each is clutching handfuls of rubbish from her trolley. Ethel is in full spate.**)

ETHEL   Now I've got these pictures to send off to my husband's brother. He's in mining you know. Married a very pretty girl, but she's not given him any children, poor dear.

CARLTON   I really wanted to be a vet.

ARLENE   Why didn't you?

CARLTON   You need 'O' level sciences. Two of them. I could have passed.

ETHEL   *(Finding an old jar)* Now she used to take this in her bath. But of course she had style. And it wasn't easy, all that roughness went against the grain, you see, she wasn't used to making allowances.

ARLENE   My dad said I'd need 'A' levels to be a nurse.

CARLTON   Thought you hated your dad.

ARLENE   Well I did.

ETHEL   Of course she had no choice in the end. It was either that dreadful admin. man from Shell or the exotic little artist from Tropical Supplies. Well that would never have done, not with her background, and she knew it.

CARLTON	But not all the time?
ARLENE	He's not so bad.
CARLTON	So all that stuff about burning his shed down . . .
ARLENE	Accident really.
CARLTON	So he's not a bastard surveyor?
ARLENE	More a surveyor than a bastard, I suppose.
CARLTON	Then why were you done in court?
ARLENE	Stupid really, took his car, ran away with this bloke. We were under age. Crashed.
CARLTON	Which bloke?
ARLENE	He was a nutter.
CARLTON	Then why'd you go with him?
ARLENE	Don't know.
CARLTON	Would you come out with me?
ETHEL	Please don't lose these. They must arrive by the first post on Friday.
ARLENE	But we've missed the post, Ethel. Went hours ago.
ETHEL	Don't be foolish, there's two more yet.
CARLTON	Would you?
ARLENE	Depends.
CARLTON	On what?
ARLENE	You'll have to take this back now, Ethel. We've got to go.
ETHEL	Only a few more minutes, just while I find . . .
CARLTON	End of the month. We've finished. Would you?
ARLENE	Yeah, why not!
CARLTON	Great . . . now Ethel, we have got to go.

(He plunges his junk back into the trolley and gets hold of Arlene's hand. There is some confusion as Ethel is trying to unpack. Laughter and they manage to kiss. SPRATCHETT comes on with Nigel.)

SPRATCHETT   LEAVE THAT WOMAN ALONE!

(There is some confusion as to exactly whom he's referring to. Nigel assumes Ethel.)

NIGEL   It's all right, Ethel's always doing that.

SPRATCHETT   Leave her alone. Leave her alone *(almost hysterical)*.

(It finally dawns on Carlton that he means Arlene. He drops her hand.)

Nothing is safe around here. Nothing's sacred. Is she all right? Are you all right?

ETHEL   You've got me flustered – I had it here a minute ago. Here, can you help me?

SPRATCHETT   *(No longer open to Ethel's demands)* I'll not have it in my park. It's not natural and I'll not have it. Barrows, get this woman out of here. And you two . . . God *(to Arlene)* you should know better. What'll your father say?

ARLENE   I don't care. Come on Carlton, let's get out of here. It must be lunch-time.

SPRATCHETT   What about your family? Think of them. I don't know. Nothing makes sense any more. No one seems to care.

(He goes off, still ranting. He is clearly close to a breakdown. Sid works. The Man in the Black Coat waits. Enter a TEACHER – she has brought her class, including KEVIN, BRIAN, LEN, to the park. She is trying to lose them.)

KEVIN   Are you sure this is allowed, Miss?

TEACHER   Don't come the righteous with me, Kevin.

KEVIN   It can't be right Miss. You're meant to be educating us. Preparing us for the harsh realities, not taking us to the park.

TEACHER   Kevin, you know full well there are two weeks to the exams, which neither you nor your friends will be taking, so why can't you just make yourself scarce?

(She is tired and lies down on the grass in the sun.)

LEN   But Miss, it says 'Do Not Walk on the Grass'.

TEACHER   I'm not walking, I'm lying, so please stop pestering me.

BRIAN   What do you want us to do?

TEACHER   Since you've left your questionnaire behind and there aren't any more tape recorders because someone has 'borrowed' the two mikes I had in my cupboard – don't bother to look innocent Kevin, I'm not looking – you'll just have to get out and observe.

BRIAN   Observe what, Miss?

TEACHER   Life's rich tapestry.

LEN   Life's rich what?

TEACHER   Watch the people come and go – talking of Michelangelo . . . but please leave me alone.

KEVIN   Hard night, Miss?

TEACHER   Hardly.

LEN   Here Kev. *(He points to the bike chained to the bench.)*

KEVIN   Nice one.

(With considerable precision they lift the bench and bike off into the trees. Meanwhile Sid digs. The Man watches. He coughs.)

MAN   Excuse me, Madam.

TEACHER   Yes?

MAN   Are you aware that those pupils in your charge have just stolen that bicycle?

TEACHER   Have they? Where?

MAN   Over there.

TEACHER   Oh God . . . KEVIN.

(She goes off in search of the boys. Sid stops and gets out a sandwich. He eats, admiring his handiwork. The Man waits. Enter PC and WPC, relaxed shirt-sleeves order. They are followed by Ethel, who is flustered.)

ETHEL   It's no good now, I'm all in a fluster. I don't know what got into him. The slightest thing sets him off. I've not seen his wretched binoculars.

(Re-enter Teacher, Kevin, Brian and Len.)

TEACHER   But that man saw you take it.

KEVIN   Couldn't be us Miss, what would we do with a bicycle? Eh Bri?

BRIAN   We was observing, Miss.

LEN   Ducks, Miss.

BRIAN   Funny habits, ducks.

TEACHER   Look, for God's sake, just put the damn thing back and we can forget all about it.

PC   Anything the matter, Miss?

TEACHER   Oh . . . er . . . yes officer, these boys . . .

KEVIN   Miss! *(Imploring.)*

TEACHER   Oh no . . . never mind.

PC   Are you sure?

TEACHER   Yes, yes, thank you. Boys, I think it's time we went back to school. It's way past the end of the lesson. Thank you, officer. Come on. **(She goes off with the boys.)**

(Shaking his head, the PC takes out his notebook and makes a note. He turns to the WPC who is rubbing her eye.)

PC   What's wrong with you?

WPC   Something in my eye.

PC   Hurt?

WPC   Not much. But I can't see a thing. Did those boys nick a bike or what?

PC   I don't know, but I wouldn't trust that teacher. Got it all wrong she has. DON'T rub it!

WPC   There's something in the corner. **(She moves in closer.)** Can you see anything?

(The PC backs away.)

PC   No . . . it's just red.

WPC   You'll not see anything from there. Could you please look properly. It's beginning to hurt.

PC   *(Reluctant to get too close)* I'm not sure . . . I can't . . .

WPC   You'll just have to touch me, Constable. It's all in the line of duty.

PC   Well hold still then, I'll see if . . . yes, there it is. I'll just see if I can . . .

(This scene is interrupted by PETE and DENISE.)

PETE   Woo hey! - Get in there, copper.

DENISE   That's pornographic, book her . . .

PETE   Getting your leg over, are you, sunshine?

(The two PCs are flustered. Pete and Denise are enjoying it. Suddenly the Man, who became agitated at the sight of Pete, leaps up. He grabs a spade and leaps at Pete. He is screaming.)

MAN   You little bastard. I've waited to get you. I'll make you pay, even if they don't.

(There is a scuffle. Denise is knocked over. Pete can't defend himself. The two PCs rush in. Sid panics - he reacts as if the violence is directed against him. He rushes off and meets Jo, who calms him.)

PETE   *(Panicking)* Get him off me. For . . .

(There is chaos, then the PCs get hold of the Man who is spent and whimpering. Denise is looking after Pete, who is gashed.)

DENISE   What was all that about?

PETE   I dunno . . . he's barmy.

DENISE   But he was after you. Why you?

PETE   I said I dunno, do I?

WPC   Now calm down, sir.

PC   Take it easy.

MAN   It was worth it . . . did I get him? Smash him?

PC   Luckily for you sir, the boy's all right.

(The man lunges up again.)

PC	Now don't be stupid. You're in enough trouble already.
WPC	Can you tell us what it's all about? It might help.
MAN	He was one of them. One of those . . . animals, that did it.
WPC	Did what?
MAN	To my Barry. They did it. And they got him, on the common, just because he was different. But they . . .
WPC	They what?
MAN	Attacked him. Kicked him half to death.
WPC	What? When?
MAN	On the common. He was just walking and him and his gang, they attacked him. And they kicked and smashed him, and they ran . . .
WPC	When was this?
MAN	Only last year, and they didn't even go to prison. Digging a garden . . . what sort of punishment's that? We're the one's that's punished – looking after him. Can't walk on his own any more. The wife's with him all the time . . .
PC	Oh God!
WPC	What?
PC	I remember. The 'queer bashing case' on Winsley Common.
MAN	Just because he was different you see. They let 'em off. They wouldn't even allow my wife in court. I told her, I told my wife, I'll get them! And when I saw him here . . .
PC	Come along. You'd better come with us.
MAN	*(As he is taken out)* But I'll get him. Don't you worry son. This ain't the end of it. Not by a long chalk.
DENISE	Is that right?
PETE	Eh?
DENISE	Is that right?
PETE	Kind of.

DENISE   Were you on that 'queer bashing' business? He was brain-damaged, wasn't he? What do you mean 'kind of'?

PETE   It wasn't like that. There were ten of us. It wasn't just me.

DENISE   But Pete, ten of you, onto one bloke. Why let 'em do it?

PETE   We were mates see. Used to go round together. Up on the common, for a lark mostly, catching lovers at it. Then we'd take the mick out of the nancies. Call 'em names and all that. Push 'em about a bit sometimes. And then this once it went too far.

DENISE   Too far? How'd you mean, it went too far? Why didn't you stop it?

PETE   Once it had started, you didn't know what was happening, see, you couldn't think. We were all . . . lost . . . together. I couldn't stop it. I daren't . . . *(Pause)* Can you understand that Denise? I hardly touched him myself. We were all caught.

DENISE   But you could have stopped them! He might as well be dead now!

PETE   Yeah. Let's go.

WPC   *(To Pete and Denise)* Can I have your names and addresses?

(The WPC leads off Pete. Denise follows. Meanwhile Jo has been comforting Sid, who is still shivering.)

JO   It's all right. It's all right. They've gone now. Why not get back to the plants. There's plenty to do. I'll give you a hand with the weeding.

(Sid is coaxed back to the flower bed. But his nerve has gone and he tramples a plant.)

I think we'd better get you back to the home. Come on. **(She leads him off.)**
(Pause.)

(Donald jogs on. He is sweating. The buzzer is going on his digital watch. He looks for the bench, does a double-take, looks again. He swears and strides off. Enter Nigel. He is nervous, looking at his watch. He rehearses.)

NIGEL   It looks like a lovely evening, why don't you and I . . .
Oh no. I need a better intro than that, straight out of
Barbara Cartland that is. Hi . . . can I walk to the gate
with you . . . would you like an ice cream? I think I can
persuade her to open, privileges of the job . . . don't cha
know! Ho, ho, ho bloody ho. This is crazy. I'll just have
to say it. Look, I've been watching you come through this
park every day for the last six months, and I really fancy
you, so could we just get it together and . . .

(This is interrupted by SUSIE. **She jogs, wearing a track suit,
with Donald following.)**

DONALD   And the thing was locked onto the bloody bench. Would
you believe it?

SUSIE   *(Smiling as she jogs by)* Hello.

**(Nigel gapes, tries to begin, begins a tentative jog along with her
to begin his spiel.)**

NIGEL   Hello . . . I've been watching you . . . I was wondering
. . .

(Susie and Donald jog off. Nigel gives up.)

Oh shit . . . who wants to get involved with a fitness freak
anyway?

(He picks up the tools and wanders off. Blackout.)

SCENE 2   It is dark. ETHEL **sleeps under a pile of newspapers. Sounds of
distant sirens.**

**(The sounds of three kids escaping and enjoying it. They rush
across stage, followed at quite a distance by** SPRATCHETT. **He is
shaking feebly. He is desperately short of breath and collapses
onto the bench.)**

SPRATCHETT   *(Wheezing heavily)* Little bastards . . . sods. If I ever get
my hands on those sodding kids, I'll nail them to the
bleedin' tree and then kick their . . . *(a burst of
wheezing).* I've had enough. I've had my fill. Hooligans

on the rampage, couldn't give a monkey's. Doesn't matter who it is, they'll trample over you. Well if I catch the little bleeders, I'll not bother with the police, their hands are tied, I'll . . . I'll get the dog on them. Make a little mistake . . . set the flamin' dog on them . . . that'd do it. Christ, I've had enough. I just don't understand it no more. It gets worse every day and no one cares . . . cares enough to do anything about it. But we're the ones that suffer, not those poncey social workers with their university degrees and pampering the little bastards. It's us, public at large, the unprotected majority, who're up against the wall, and we can't take it much longer. I'm not taking it any more. Take the law into my own hands . . . only way . . .

(A figure rushes through, yelling. Spratchett leaps up.)

COME HERE! . . . *(Collapses onto the bench, wheezing.)* Oh Christ, what's the use of trying to make a stand? You get laughed at these days trying to make a stand for what's right and decent and . . . normal. Old fashioned. Yeah, it's old fashioned to care about decency and honesty and standards. Well, I am bloody old fashioned and proud of it. I don't care who knows it.

(Pause.)

'Course the brass up in head office, they don't like you to be old fashioned. Oh no, they don't want a fuss from any old insignificant park keeper. Just keep your head down and your nose clean until retirement Alf, there's a good lad. No matter that the park's full of hippies, hooligans, loonies and perverts, just keep the place tidy and don't make a fuss. They just don't understand what it's like down here. They sit in their comfy office and hope that it'll go away. Well it won't, not now it won't, not these days. It's a bloody mess and nobody gives a damn.

(Pause.)

Christ, it was different when I was a lad. You knew where you were. No skulking in alleys to get old ladies with a broken bottle and an ammonia spray. We took it then, we didn't harbour nasty little grudges. And there was the army, the war. No bloody time for asking questions, being confused. We got in there and did what we were told. We were proud, oh, we were proud to be British. Christ, those were the days. You really knew where you were . . .

(Silence. He broods, then quietly at first, gathering strength, he enacts a parade-ground scene.)

Company . . . company . . . SHUN . . . shoulder arms . . . up two, three, across two, three, down two, three. General salute . . . Present . . . ARMS . . . hup two, three, slap two, three, down two, three.

(Standing rigid in the present-arms position, he begins to hum the National Anthem. As he is doing this, Ethel emerges. He sees her, turns, alarmed and panicked.)

Who's that? Stand back! Get off me . . . *(He recognises her.)* Oh, it's you. What the hell are you doing here? The park's closed. You should have gone. You can't stay here.

ETHEL My husband was in the army, you know.

SPRATCHETT I asked you what in God's name you are doing in my park at this time of night?

ETHEL He was killed at Monte Casino.

SPRATCHETT Stop gibbering woman, and get out.

ETHEL Killed by his own shells. 'Error of judgement', they said. 'Deepest regrets.' Said he was a fine soldier and a gentleman. Not much good to me that, when all's said and done.

SPRATCHETT I'm not telling you again. Move out of here!

(He begins to jostle her.)

ETHEL He used to like parades. I remember one afternoon on the parade ground at Aldershot. We were all invited. Hats and gloves too.

(She is packing up her newspapers.)

SPRATCHETT Leave that rubbish behind.

ETHEL A beautiful afternoon. A beautiful parade. The old Queen Mary was giving medals. One of the young men had no legs.

SPRATCHETT	Stop ranting, woman.
ETHEL	Beautiful boy. Can't have been more than twenty.
SPRATCHETT	GET OUT OF MY PARK. MOVE! YOU BLOODY LOONY.
ETHEL	*(She finally begins to go.)* They gave him a medal, though; he seemed happy with that.

(She finally goes off.)

SPRATCHETT   Should be locked away, she's a disgrace to the human race, she is. Just left to rot in the park in full view of everyone. That's where the welfare state gets you. Loonies in the park scaring the life out of law-abiding citizens. Drivelling away. Dribbling away.

(He is wheezing again and collapses back onto the bench. He falls silent, then begins to get the spooks.)

What's that? Who's there? Can't see 'em, Who's there? Must be blacks, can't see 'em in the dark. Look for the whites of their eyes. Huh! *(He turns.)* Get off me. We've had enough from your lot. You lot started the rot. We respect our women, don't treat them like animals. Oh yes, I know what they say, but what does it matter if you haven't got a brain in your head?

Now you lot, don't skulk around in the shadows. I know you're there. Come and get me if you dare. I'm not scared of the likes of you. I'm British stock, you'll not take me without a fight. Come on you black bastards, FIGHT.

(He wheels about. He picks up the litter bin to protect himself.)

I know I'm outnumbered, but they're the odds you like, aren't they?

Come on. I said come out here where I can see you. COME OUT HERE YOU SWINE.

(He is frozen with the litter bin held over his head. Silence. He slowly lowers the bin. Whimpering, he leaves.)

End of Act Two

ACT THREE

SCENE 1   Eighteen months have passed. It is autumn. Leaves are all over the ground. NORRIS, LEN, BRIAN are in overalls. They are working in the garden. In the background, and it will be in the background to most of the scene, we hear the sounds of a police operation. Sirens, the odd indistinguishable sound of a loud-hailer, the crackle of radio static, etc. During the scene it will intrude periodically, but it must always be there. REG is teaching Norris to prune. Len and Brian are sweeping leaves.

LEN   This is so bloody boring.

BRIAN   Leaves, leaves, leaves.

LEN   Hey, Reg, why'd you stick with a job like this? You're respectable, responsible . . .

NORRIS   . . . and you white brother!

LEN   Can't understand why you stick it . . . the dirt, the weather.

REG   Careful with those secateurs lad, we don't want to kill it do we?

BRIAN   You gonna kill 'em anyway. Slashing 'em down like that.

REG   Don't you believe it. You come back next spring and . . .

NORRIS   We will!

REG   Yes, well, next year it'll all be new growth off those stems. Strong and green, but . . . NOT THERE! Look, take all the leaders off that one . . . that's it. Don't mess about with that central one – that's the main stem, it's the way down to the roots.

NORRIS   Gotta have roots, heh Reg?

(Len and Brian are larking about.)

REG   That's right, now gently . . . you see all that can go, it's had its day. Look at the suckers all over it.

LEN   Gotta be cruel to be kind.

REG   Afraid so.

(DONALD rides in on a third bike. He has two chains draped over his shoulder and another one is draped over the bike. The lads stop working and watch as he solemnly chains the bike to a tree with the two chains. Each lock needs a different key. As he finishes, SUSIE jogs on in a track suit. She carries yet another chain.)

DONALD   Thank you, darling.

SUSIE   It's very heavy, darling.

DONALD   I know, darling, I'm sorry.

SUSIE   But darling, does it really need three chains?

DONALD   'Fraid so, darling.

SUSIE   Wouldn't two be enough?

DONALD   *(As he carefully pockets the keys)* Better safe than sorry, eh, darling?

(They go off holding hands, jogging in a rather exaggerated way.)

LEN   Better safe than sorry . . .

BRIAN   Daaarling!

NORRIS   White trash.

REG   Now then . . . let's get on with it.

(They work. There is a burst of activity from the police. A siren, an indistinct order on the loud-hailer.)

LEN   What is all that about?

BRIAN   You know, Reg?

REG   Search me.

NORRIS   The righteous is bein' persecuted.

(They work.)

LEN   But really, Reg, why you do this job?

REG   Steady business, gardening. You don't get many surprises and you know where you are. There's an order to it all. That's reassuring. If you work in a garden, you don't get frightened by changes.

(NIGEL wheels in SPRATCHETT. He is in a wheelchair. He has clearly had a breakdown. He is dressed in a black blazer with a regimental crest. Nigel now wears the park keeper's hat and suit.)

NIGEL   It's good to have you back, Mr Spratchett. We were wondering how you'd been getting on. I meant to get round to see you, but with all the extra work . . .

SPRATCHETT   I'm surprised they gave the job to you. Needs experience. Took me years before I was ready for that kind of responsibility. Experience doesn't count for much these days.

NIGEL   Don't you believe it. There's been many a time when I've needed advice. *(He has stopped the wheelchair.)* Will this do then?

SPRATCHETT   Suppose it'll have to.

NIGEL   Are you sure that you'll be warm enough? *(He sees Spratchett's lapel badge.)* Hello, what's this? You've joined the Front have you?

SPRATCHETT   You mean the National Front Party of Great Britain. I certainly have. And not before time, whatever you may say. They've got the best policies.

NIGEL   What rubbish. Their policies stink. They're a con. Tricking people by encouraging their nastiest fears.

SPRATCHETT   That's just propaganda, lad. How much do you know about their policies? On housing, rates, taxes, transport?

NIGEL   That's just a smoke screen for . . .

SPRATCHETT   'Course, you don't know a thing about it. Haven't bothered to find out. Duped by the communist fifth-column. Our people are the only ones with the guts to face up to the real cause of the trouble today. Someone's got to make a stand before it's too late. I mean, take the

blacks *(motioning to Norris)*. The country can't afford
them, taking our jobs, sponging off social security. You
can't call this country a British nation any more.

NIGEL   That simply isn't true. All you've got to do is look at the
figures . . .

SPRATCHETT   Don't try and argue with figures. Look at the facts.
Millions of them. They got no discipline and they think
we owe them a living. We've got to have some discipline,
it's the only way we'll survive against the international
financiers. Send them home and we've got a chance.

NIGEL   How'd it happen then?

SPRATCHETT   I'm not saying it'll be easy. Bound to be nasty, but they
deserve it, don't they? What they ever done for this
country? No, we'll just ship them out then . . .

NIGEL   No. I mean how'd you get to join? Six months ago you
wouldn't have anything to do with them. Extremists, you
said then, said they were too violent.

SPRATCHETT   Ah, well I was wrong, wasn't I? Victim of the media's
propaganda. They're only violent when they have to
defend themselves against the commie thugs.

NIGEL   But when did you join?

SPRATCHETT   Well, after my . . . illness. You know, I'd just got back
from the hospital, just been pensioned off. Well, they
came round to my flat. They'd heard about my argument
with the Paki doctor. Really sympathetic they were,
cheered me up. Then we talked. They explained. I
understood it a lot better then.

NIGEL   Ah, well, you would've, wouldn't you?

SPRATCHETT   Thing is, a lot of their policies, I'd been thinking that
way for some time.

NIGEL   That's not true. You may have been a bit old fashioned
for effect, but you never went that far.

SPRATCHETT   Maybe not in front of you, but it was in my mind, I
assure you. Now, I do a lot of committee work.

NIGEL	Keep you busy do they?
SPRATCHETT	Not half. There's so much to do. Especially with elections coming up. We're going for the young voters this time. And then there's the new HQ down Brick Lane. We're really making progress.
NIGEL	Well you're bound to make progress, of a sort. There must be plenty more like you, nowhere to go, nothing to do except brood on their petty insecurities.
SPRATCHETT	Who's petty?
NIGEL	Still, I can't hang around here all day putting you straight. I have things to do, people to see. I'll leave you here, if that's all right. You can talk to Reg and the lads, if you get bored.
SPRATCHETT	You'll come and get me if you need me?
NIGEL	'Course I will.
SPRATCHETT	I can still do the paper work, make myself useful.
NIGEL	I'll let you know if there's anything. *(He moves off past Reg and the lads.)* Everything OK, Reg?
REG	The lads were wondering, Nigel, what's all the noise about?
NIGEL	Police, there must be fifty of them, with cars, radios, the lot.
NORRIS	Babylon.
NIGEL	There's some sort of a siege going on.
REG	What, terrorists?
NIGEL	No, just some nut in a council flat. He's got an old lady up there and I think it's a shot gun. Won't come down.
SPRATCHETT	Snipers. They should use snipers.
NIGEL	I don't think it's quite like that, Mr Spratchett.
REG	How long's it been going on then?
NIGEL	Molly says it started just after I left last night.
REG	Been going all night then?
NIGEL	Must have been. They've blocked off Milden Lane.

LEN   What's he done, this guy?

NIGEL   Nothing much, just won't come down.

REG   Must have cracked.

NIGEL   I should imagine so . . . **(He goes off.)**

REG   Morning, Mr Spratchett. Feeling any better?

SPRATCHETT   Much the same, thank you.

                 (They work. The lads are very sullen in Spratchett's presence.)

                 Pst, Reg, here a minute.

REG   Half a mo, Alf.

SPRATCHETT   No, now, here a minute.

                 (Reg reluctantly goes over.)

REG   What is it?

SPRATCHETT   *(Pointing to Norris)* That one . . . he's giving me the eye.

REG   Ignore it Alf. He's all right.

SPRATCHETT   No, they do that, you know. Look at you funny. It's their way. *(In a conspiratorial way)* Not having any trouble, are you Reg? With him?

REG   No, no, Mr Spratchett, he's working hard.

SPRATCHETT   Well, he would be, the darky. He would, wouldn't he? Takes 'em back you see . . .

REG   Well I don't know about that, but I've had no trouble.

SPRATCHETT   Well you jus' watch 'im. Don't turn your back on 'im if you can help it and watch the eyes. There – he's doing it again. Here you, blackie, stop that.

NORRIS   Shut your rarse.

REG   All right Norris. Ignore it, please.

NORRIS   You're no better, talking to him.

REG   Norris, take that rake and go and rake that approach lawn that Mr Barrows was talking about. Go on now.

(Norris does so, reluctantly, muttering abuse.)

Come on, Alf, let's move you over here and you can keep an eye on the siege.

SPRATCHETT   You don't have to treat me like a child, you know.

REG   No, I don't *have* to . . . There you are.

(**Spratchett is facing away from the lads, in a corner. They work. Enter** ETHEL. **She is looking for something.**)

ETHEL   I've got to find those keys . . . it's too late even now . . . He'll be so angry. He gave them to me specially, to look after.

(**She approaches Spratchett. He is clearly embarrassed by his vulnerability. He tries to ignore her.**)

You don't remember where I put those keys, do you? I'm late for my appointment already and he'll not understand what it's like.

(**She wanders past Spratchett, who is visibly relieved, and approaches Reg.**)

Would you mind looking down by your feet? They could have dropped anywhere here, it's so urgent. He'll only cancel the trip, and then where'll I be? Please look . . . and you, they could easily be over there.

REG   They're not here Ethel, sorry.

(**She goes off, past Spratchett, who cringes. As she goes off,** CARLTON **comes on. He is wearing a rather worn suit, a little too small for him, and a tie. Norris accompanies him.**)

CARLTON   Morning Ethel. How you keepin'?

ETHEL   I'm off to find my keys.

CARLTON   Good luck to you, dear. Morning Mr Spratshit, heard about your breakdown.

SPRATCHETT   Stroke!

CARLTON   Better now? You're looking well. Got some colour in your cheeks!

NORRIS   Colour in your cheeks!

CARLTON   Hi, Reg.

NORRIS   So what you doin' now?

CARLTON   Well, I don't want to be too excited, but I think just maybe I got a job interview this afternoon. Working for the NSPCC, 'orderly' to start with, then plenty of 'opportunity for advancement'.

BRIAN   What's the NSPC whatsit?

LEN   It's the Cruelty. Stoppin' dolts like you thumpin' their kids.

CARLTON   No, well it won't be that, it'll be working in their hospital.

NORRIS   Cleanin' up shit, I suppose. Emptyin' rubbish. 'Opportunity for advancement' my rarse.

CARLTON   It's not like that Norris. It's not like an ordinary hospital.

NORRIS   Dey say, dey say! They got you, Carlton . . . Interview, ha! You don't need an interview to clean shit.

REG   So when is this interview, then?

CARLTON   One o'clock, Reg. I jus' come round to say that I used your name as a reference. Is that OK?

REG   Fine. Will they be in touch with me or should I . . .

CARLTON   Well, I gave them the address of the park office, so it should get to you here.

REG   I'd be glad to give you a reference, lad, and I hope you get the job. Optimistic are you?

CARLTON   Well, I've learnt never to be that, nowadays, but yes, the bloke was very helpful and . . .

NORRIS   Cleanin' up kids' shit, huh!

REG   And how's Arlene? See much of her, do you, these days?

CARLTON   Not much, no . . .

REG   Gone off you has she, or did you find yourself another?

CARLTON   Not exactly. It was her dad . . .

REG   Oh?

CARLTON	Well, I never met him, but that's what she said. She said he'd never talk to her again if it went on – so she couldn't see me any more.
REG	She gave me the impression she hated his guts and wouldn't care a damn what he thought.
CARLTON	Yeah, well, that's what I thought, but it wasn't quite like that somehow.
REG	I thought there was something funny there.
CARLTON	I don't know – all I know is I don't see her these days.
REG	Plenty more fish in the sea . . .
CARLTON	Stick with my own kind, you mean.
REG	I didn't say that.
CARLTON	No, but I'm beginning to think it's good advice. With her I thought it was different . . . anyway, see you Reg, and thanks.
REG	Best of luck, and let us know how it goes.
NORRIS	See you soon, Carlton!
CARLTON	Bye . . . *(He sees the bike.)* I see the jogger king's not taking any chances. Bye Reg.

(Carlton goes off. They work. Norris chuckles to himself. On his way out, Carlton meets MRS WALTON. *She now looks austere and drained. She hardly recognises him.)*

CARLTON	Why, Mrs Walton. How you bin? How's that Selwyn boy then? Still kickin' up a ruckus?
MRS WALTON	Hello. You lookin' smart. Mekin' something outta yourself?
CARLTON	Giving it a try. It hurts, though. So how's Selwyn?
MRS WALTON	I don' know. What you doin' then?
CARLTON	Me, oh lookin' for a job. Got an interview today. What you mean 'don't know'?
MRS WALTON	What I say. Don' know and don' care. He's not my boy no more.

CARLTON   What you mean?

MRS WALTON   We give 'im everything an' he just leave us. We glad to
             see 'im go.

CARLTON   But where is he now? I mean, do you see 'im at all?

MRS WALTON   Who knows? Prison maybe. I ain't seen 'im for six
             months. Heard nothin' neither.

             (Pause.)

             Me daughter doin' fine now. Gotta job in the city.
             Makin' good money. Why don't you come round some
             time, meet her?

CARLTON   Yeah, well I'll do that . . . I must be off now. I'm sorry
             about Selwyn.

MRS WALTON   Don' be sorry. We're not. It's his life he's wastin'. I've
             washed me hands of 'im a long time ago.

CARLTON   I suppose so. I'm still sorry. Anyway, I must go, I'll be
             late.

MRS WALTON   Good luck chil'.

             **(They both go off. MAGGIE comes on carrying a clip board. She
             is talking to DENISE, who is wheeling a pram.)**

MAGGIE   So how old is he now?

DENISE   Almost six months.

MAGGIE   He's big, isn't he?

DENISE   He's a hell of a weight, already. Carrying him up all
             those steps. Gawd knows what he'll be like in a year's
             time.

MAGGIE   How are you managing?

DENISE   OK, I suppose. I'm still trying to find a nursery that'll
             take 'im. They say he's too young.

MAGGIE   What about the father?

DENISE   I still see him, but, I don't know. He can't make up his
             mind. Says it makes him feel 'claustrophobic'.

MAGGIE   Yes, it usually does when you've got the choice. You're
             better off rid of a bloke like that. They're all the same,
             mind you.

DENISE	Oh, I don't know. I still like him, really. It's just that he's not ready for this sort of responsibility, I suppose.
MAGGIE	And are you?
DENISE	Haven't got much option, have I?
MAGGIE	No. That's my point. Still, sounds to me as if you're coping very well. Drop round the home for a cuppa. We'd love to see you, both.
DENISE	Thanks Maggie. I'll see you then. Ta ta. *(She wheels the pram past the lads and Reg.)* Hi, Reg.
REG	Hello Denise. How's your little girl?
DENISE	Boy, actually, and he's fine. See you. **(She wheels the pram off.)**
MAGGIE	Everything all right, Reg?
REG	Fine. All working hard.
MAGGIE	Even old Norris? That's good news. What do you think of it so far, Norris?
	(Norris ignores her.)
	Be like that. What about you, Len? Outdoor life appeal to you?
LEN	S'all right.
MAGGIE	Go on, you love it, really. Any complaints, Brian?
BRIAN	Yeah, Reg. He keeps beating me up for no reason. I want a transfer.
MAGGIE	Oh that's fine, as long as there aren't any bruises.
BRIAN	You've got no heart, Miss.
MAGGIE	Got to be cruel to be kind, Brian. Cheerio Reg, see you lot this evening and no dawdling on the way back.
	(She leaves them. WENDELL, KEVIN, SYLVAN come on. They are wearing greasy overalls. They have jobs, but the jobs are menial. They are carrying copies of *The Sun* **and lunch bags.)**
LEN	Don't tell me they been nicked too!

NORRIS	They's not been nicked – they's workin'. Job creation scheme. Don't sound too different to me.
WENDELL	I tell you this bird had on a bikini.
KEVIN	What, in October?
WENDELL	Well, I said it might have been a couple of weeks back.
KEVIN	Still, worth coming here. Eye up the talent.
WENDELL	'Ere you know Wheeler? He's watchin' you. I noticed. First opportunity and pow! You'll be out. He's gotta nephew left school July, he wants him in the job.
KEVIN	Well he can have the soddin' job.
WENDELL	Not mine, man. OK for you. Jobs hard to come by for de bredaren, The money's OK, get off early on Fridays if he's in a good mood. At least it's a job.
KEVIN	But it's so bloody boring and the noise is driving me barmy.

(Another burst of activity from the siege)

SYLVAN	Heh, hear that. Still some action other side of the park.
KEVIN	Here, let's go over, see what's up. Maybe some blood. Make a change from page three.
WENDELL	They said some nutter's up there goin' kill an ol' lady.
KEVIN	Sounds tasty.

(They trot off. As they go, they bump into PETE, who is dressed in a snappy Burton's suit, with wide lapels. He has ARLENE on his arm. She is clearly his doll, and is acting 'engaged'. The lads bump into him and whistle up Arlene.)

PETE	Piss off you greasy sods. Mind the suit!
ARLENE	What do they look like?
PETE	Ugly and uncouth. Not your sort, I hope.
ARLENE	Not on your life.
PETE	And what have we hear . . . why hello, Mr Spratchett. Had a fall have we?
SPRATCHETT	Out of my way, I can't see what's going on.

PETE   Don't worry, nothing's goin' to happen, the TV boys not arrived yet.

(Nigel walks past.)

Well, well, well. We have gone up in the world, have we not?

NIGEL   Hello Arlene, hello Pete. You seem to be doing all right yourself.

PETE   Well what is it now? Park keeper, at how old?

NIGEL   Acting *(He moves them away from Spratchett.)*

PETE   Very reasonable screw, I should imagine, must be eight thousand and then there's overtime.

NIGEL   No, no, nothing like that. How are you, Arlene?

ARLENE   Fine thanks, just fine. Did you know that me and Pete's engaged?

NIGEL   Oh, that's nice . . . congratulations.

ARLENE   Should be in the spring, if Pete gets the promotion he's expecting.

NIGEL   Oh promotion, eh? You surprise me!

PETE   Yes, I'm in Auto Parts now.

NIGEL   Oh, that's interesting, I've just got this MGB, second hand, needs . . .

PETE   Growth industry, squire. High street market's booming and the mail-order business is on the up. Can't fail.

ARLENE   Pete's a salesman, travels round this area.

PETE   I'm hoping for the Medway Area Sales Rep. Then they'll give me a Datsun Supreme, on the firm. All the trimmings.

ARLENE   Fur-lined seats, stereo tape deck and a sunshield with Pete and Arlene. They're nice those, don't you think?

PETE   Four-tone horn and a pair of big Slicks on the back. Got to advertise, you see. I'm thinking of branching out on my own soon. Alloy wheels, son, huge growth there. My mate's doing the ground work. We've got our eye on a corner shop. Can't fail.

ARLENE   Then we'll soon have enough to put down on a flat. Nothing big, enough to start a family, you know, get the first one on the way.

NIGEL   Sounds ideal! Funnily enough I saw Denise . . .

ARLENE   Then once Pete's really established, we should be able to move out to Barnet.

NIGEL   Wasn't that where your dad lived?

ARLENE   Yes, it's a very nice area, definitely on the up.

NIGEL   Depends on what you want, I suppose.

ARLENE   'Course, it's early days yet, but those are our plans. You got to think ahead, Reg taught us that, didn't he . . .

PETE   Yeah. *(He gets up and goes over to Reg.)* How's it going then, Reg? The garden, I mean . . .

REG   Oh, much the same, much the same.

PETE   Yeah, well it would. Mind you, beats me why you stick with this. A man of your experience could make a bomb for himself in marketing. Look at Percy Thrower. Ever thought about it?

REG   Among other things, but . . .

PETE   Well, if you ever think about it again, give us a bell.

ARLENE   Pete!

PETE   No, no, don't get me wrong. Early days, but I could be in a position, a few years hence, to put something your way. Sales side. You know what I mean? Anyway, we must be off. Can't stand here nattering all day. Things to do, people to see, and you are meeting your Dad for lunch. Ta ta then, Reg, Nigel. Next stop head office, eh, old son?

NIGEL	Unlikely Pete, I haven't got your drive, easily satisfied, I am. Bye Arlene, hope it works out for you.
ARLENE	Oh, it will, don't worry. Bye Reg.

(They walk off.)

NORRIS	Man, he jus' gotta have a fall comin'. He's so full o' wind and piss, he jus' gotta burst soon. He was doin' time here weren't he, Reg?
REG	That's right.
NORRIS	What he get done for? Connin' old ladies outta their gas money?
REG	No, he wasn't so independent then.

(Norris somewhat ostentatiously decides to make for the bench for a cigarette. Reg sees him and is clearly in two minds as to how to deal with it.)

REG	Where you off to?
NORRIS	Restin'.
REG	Not for long I hope, we've still got a lot to do.
NORRIS	Long as it takes.
SPRATCHETT	You're not going to let him get away with that, are you Reg? Here you, get back to work. Do as you're told.
REG	Thank you Alf. I don't need your help.

(Norris glares and Reg lets him be and returns to his work. SONIA comes on. She sees Norris and joins him on the bench.)

SONIA	Hi Norris. So you ended up back here. I heard you was sent to Church Street.
NORRIS	Better than prison.
SONIA	Too true. How they treatin' you?
NORRIS	I mekin' out.
SONIA	I hope you ain't actin' feisty, shootin' your mouth.
NORRIS	A man gotta duty to say what he believe.
SONIA	Not if a man always in trouble as a result.

NORRIS   Babylon can't stand the truth. I and I must speak out against the persecution.

SONIA   I know Norris, I know, but what you and the brethren have difficulty in realising is that we have the misfortune to live in a white country. Just pretending to be 'multi-cultural'. It's a lie because your culture ain't worth a damn thing. You gonna have to forget the truth and think about the future.

NORRIS   What future?

SONIA   OK, so it ain't easy, but the conquering lion of Judah never put any money in your pocket.

NORRIS   Maybe pride worth more than pounds an' pence.

SONIA   That's your trouble Norris, you always was too proud.

(Pause.)

NORRIS   You seen Doreen?

SONIA   Yeah. We're still friends. In fact she said she'd meet me here for lunch.

NORRIS   She gotta man?

SONIA   No one serious. You want to see her?

NORRIS   No point. *(Pause)* She still gotta job?

SONIA   Yeah, same one. She hates it, but she got no choice.

NORRIS   She gotta choice! She jus' won't take it. I tol' her to come with me, be my woman.

SONIA   Oh that 'choice'. Yeah she made that choice and you was vex because she didn't choose you.

(DOREEN comes running on from the direction of the siege.)

DOREEN   Sorry Sonia, I didn't mean to be so . . .

(She sees Norris, who has got up to go.)

Oh . . . Hi! I didn't expect to see you here . . . you all right?

(Norris returns to his work after a moment's hesitation.)

NORRIS   Just fine, how'd you think?

(Doreen is undecided whether to pursue the conversation.)

DOREEN   Sorry I'm late . . . Were you talking to him?

SONIA   Doing my best. Anyway, what made you so late?

DOREEN   Oh, I was watching this police business. They trying to get this man down from a flat. Police with guns, dogs, fire engines, everything.

SONIA   Just for one guy?

DOREEN   Come on, let's go and watch. Could be exciting.

SONIA   You haven't changed much, have you?

DOREEN   What you mean?

SONIA   At school whenever there was an accident or a fight you was always the first there.

DOREEN   I may have been first, sister, but you was there eventually. At the back of the crowd staring. I was just honest, that's all. Come on, just a look. If nothing happens we'll find a peaceful park bench and you can tell me more about this posh job.

(**They go off together. Reg and the boys work on. Donald comes past, followed by Susie. They are searching. They go up to the area round the bike.**)

DONALD   I must have dropped them here.

SUSIE   Why must you? It could have been anywhere.

DONALD   Slipped out of my pocket as I was leaving.

SUSIE   This is so stupid, Donald, why do you have to have so many damn keys anyway?

DONALD   Darling, please don't criticise, not now. We can discuss it later. *(Eyeing the lads)* You don't suppose they . . .

SUSIE   Very unlikely, and anyway, there's not much you can do about it now.

DONALD   This is ridiculous.

SUSIE   They're not here.

DONALD   I suppose I could have dropped them as I was running.

SUSIE Oh, God!

DONALD Look I'll go back over our circuit and you'd better go and ask that park keeper chap. He fancies you, he might put himself out.

SUSIE There's no need to be snarky.

DONALD Sorry darling, but it's such a damn nuisance. Don't know what we'll do if we can't find them.

(The lads work. Suddenly there is a lot of noise from the siege. Shouting, and then over the loud-hailer: 'We'll count to five, then we're coming in, one . . . two . . . three . . . four.' There is a loud explosion, more shouts, sounds of a door being broken down. More shouts and then sirens. Norris, Len and Brian run off, followed by Reg, who is protesting.)

SPRATCHETT Bloody hell, they got the bastard. I told you, didn't I? Snipers, can hit a cap badge at one hundred yards they can. That's shown 'em. That's the way to do it. Right through the window.

(Nigel runs on, followed by Susie. They meet Reg coming back.)

NIGEL What's happened, Reg? Anyone hurt?

REG I don't know. There was a shot and a lot of shouting.

SUSIE In the park?

REG No, no, outside. The siege.

NIGEL Some bloke with a gun.

(The WPC runs on.)

WPC Are you the park keeper?

SPRATCHETT Yes . . .

NIGEL Yes I am. What's the trouble, can I help?

WPC Could we use your office? We've got some casualties and we'd like to keep them apart for the moment.

NIGEL Of course, what happened?

WPC Bloke in the siege, young chap. When they put the pressure on he cracked. Fired and . . .

NIGEL	What . . . killed?
WPC	No, only wounded a policeman. Can you show me your office?
NIGEL	Yes, this way.
WPC	Could the ambulance get up there when it comes?
NIGEL	Oh yes.

(They go off. Donald wanders past, looking for his keys.)

SUSIE	For God's sake, Donald, give it a rest.
DONALD	But I've got to find them.
SUSIE	Just stop thinking about your precious bike for a moment. Something's up.
SPRATCHETT	Hey, they're bringing him this way. He's walking, can't have killed him . . . wonder what went wrong?

(The PC leads on SID, wrapped in a blanket.)

That the one, is it?

PC	Come along now, take it slowly.
SPRATCHETT	So that's the one, eh? Weedy looking specimen, isn't he?
REG	Hello, Sid.
SID	Hello, Reg.
REG	How . . . how you been?
SID	Oh, up and down, Reg, up and down.
REG	Not seen much of you since you left
SID	No.
REG	Not hurt, are you?
SID	No, not hurt.
REG	So they finally got to you then?
SID	'Fraid so.
REG	You didn't take my advice.

SID   Tried to, Reg. Tried to. But it wasn't easy, they wouldn't listen, you see. Not like you said. Different in the garden you see. I had the respect. But they were different, pushed around I was, here and there, 'Yes sir, no sir' – 'I'll try it sir' – 'I'm sorry ma'am' – and then when I tried . . . to . . . make a stand. Then this happens. *(Pause)* I didn't hurt her, Reg.

REG   'Course not, Sid.

SID   But I just had to show them.

REG   You showed them, Sid.

(Pause)

SID   Reg?

REG   Yes, Sid.

SID   When it's over, d'you think I could come back?

REG   'Course you can, Sid. Plenty to do in the garden.

SID   If I could work for you here?

REG   Might work, Sid.

SID   Got to bend with the wind, eh Reg?

REG   Best policy, lad.

SID   Best policy.

PC   Come on Sid, we better be going.

REG   Ta, ta Sid, see you soon.

SID   See you.

(The WPC returns)

WPC   Right, I'll take him from here . . . come on Sid . . .

(Maggie and JO **come on. Jo is dressed in a casual but utilitarian style.)**

JO   Poor bloke. Are you sure you can't do anything? You're my last hope. I can't seem to get anyone to take the slightest interest in him. And now this. It had to happen.

MAGGIE	No, really Jo, there's nothing we can do for him now.
JO	But he was so calm and peaceful when he was with you.
MAGGIE	I'm not saying we couldn't help, even for a second time. It's a good system. Look at you . . .
JO	A model client I'm sure.
MAGGIE	And the rest of your group that time. There's Denise, she's settling down nicely.
JO	Not much choice, has she? And what about Pete? He was a loser deep down.
MAGGIE	Not on your life. He's really going places. Engaged to Arlene, she tells me.
JO	What! I thought she had more sense.
MAGGIE	Likes the security I should imagine. He's a rising star in the retail business by all accounts.
JO	I suppose we've got to call that success, although pretty fragile in my opinion. But what about Sid? Why can't you give him another go? I'm sure he'd settle down, especially in the gardens. God knows what'll happen to him otherwise.
MAGGIE	I'm sorry Jo, I'd love to help you, I really would. But for starters he's too old now. And secondly the courts would never send him to us a second time, however much you pleaded. He's one of our failures. What they've been waiting for. For him it's back to tried and tested ways. And I better go and get those lads back to work. Maybe see you back at the home. (**She goes off.**)
REG	Hello, Jo. Did you see poor old Sid? Sad business.
JO	I'm afraid so. It was partly my responsibility.
REG	How's that?
JO	I'm a trainee social-worker. Sid's proper social worker moved up North and because I said I knew him they put me onto his case. They've still not appointed a replacement. Not much good I can do him now.
REG	I'd never have thought.

JO   Well, he's never fitted in ever since he started school . . .

REG   No, I mean you, a social worker. You seemed dead against that sort of thing when you were here.

JO   Oh, I don't know. It's difficult to tell what you really think, anyhow I'm not sure this job's got much future. Not if Sid's anything to go by.

(She moves to go.)

REG   Jo, don't give up on him . . . They've been doing that for years.

JO   I'll try not to, I'll do my best, however much good that'll do him.

REG   I thought you would, and if there's anything I can do to help . . .

JO   Tell you something.

REG   What's that.

JO   That flat of theirs, it had some beautiful window boxes. Even now, this time of year. Full of green and colour.

REG   Yes, well he would have. He had a good touch with plants. He understood their ways.

JO   Bye Reg.

REG   Bye Jo, look after yourself.

(She goes off.)

SPRATCHETT   Window boxes! Grievous bodily harm, that's what he'll be up for, and all she can talk about is window boxes!

REG   Not a million miles apart, Alf. Not a million miles .

(Norris wanders back on his own.)

Ah, Norris. I'm taking Mr Spratchett back to the park keeper's house. Will you take those tools back to the shed and I'll meet you at the mower shed. We'll do the lawn this afternoon.

SPRATCHETT   Reg! You're not letting him take those tools?

REG   Give it a rest, Alf. He's a good lad. Coming on well. A little less of your aggravation and he'll turn out fine.

(He begins to wheel him off.)

SPRATCHETT   They've had all the chances they deserve, and more . . . It's time someone had the courage to draw the line.

REG   And that's what you're doing, eh Alf?

SPRATCHETT   That's what I tried Reg, I tried to make a stand.

REG   You could say that.

SPRATCHETT   I am saying it. I am. Show them what's right and what's wrong. Rub their noses in it. They'll soon learn.

REG   I doubt it, Alf. Somehow I doubt it.

(Reg wheels him off.)

(Donald crosses the stage, searching. He goes up to his bike, contemplates a feeble attempt to extract the bike from its chains, gives up in disgust and stamps off. Enter Ethel. As usual she is searching.)

ETHEL   I'm quite sure I had them. Clear as crystal. I remember putting them down and saying: 'Ethel, don't forget the keys, you'll be needing them soon', and then all those interruptions. Visitors and tradespeople, all wanting something. And now if I don't find them, I shan't know what to do. That desk has got all my documents, and I'll need them for the next . . . she'll never forgive me . . . there they are.

(She picks up the bicycle keys from the grass.)

I knew I wasn't wrong. I knew I'd find them in the end. Just keep looking, that's my policy, because once you get in a panic . . . Now I must rush, because he'll be waiting, and now I've got the key, it'll be all right, I'm sure of that. **(She wanders off.)**

(Lights slowly down, leaving the bike, chained up, for a moment before Blackout.)

THE MAKING OF THE PLAY

Roots, Rules and Tribulation was specially written for a particular group of young people, between the ages of fourteen and twenty-one, who lived in North London and had joined the Cockpit Youth Theatre. The actors were all used to working with each other and I had got to know them before I began to write the play. Many of the parts were written with particular actors in mind. For instance, the part of Norris was written for a West Indian member of the group whose ideas were very close to those of Norris in the play. Unfortunately, half way through rehearsals he decided to leave London and join a Rastafarian commune in Wales. Perhaps I should have finished the play with Norris doing the same thing.

Not only did I know the actors I would be writing for, but I also had a very clear idea of the audience that would be seeing the play. *Roots* had to interest the young people who lived in the area around the theatre. It had to have humour they could understand and enjoy, but it also had to deal with some of the important issues in their lives. I felt that young people were fed up with being talked down to and that they did not want to see a play which told them what to think. I hoped that *Roots* would entertain them, but also make them think about their own opinions.

I chose to write about punishment because at that time the government was talking a lot about 'short, sharp shocks' for young offenders. I wanted *Roots* to suggest that there were alternatives to the 'short, sharp shock' treatment. I certainly believe that the alternative described in the play is likely to do a great deal more good than the 'short, sharp shock', but I wanted the play to show the weaknesses of the community-care system as well as its strengths. At the time of writing there was also a lot of concern about the 'sus' laws, which allowed the police to pick up anyone 'on suspicion that they might be about to commit a crime'. Many young people were particularly angry about the way the law was being used to arrest young black people without any reason. The law has now been changed, but at that time it was an important issue.

Most of the play was written before rehearsals began, although bits were added and other bits taken out as the actors worked on their parts. The girls who played Doreen and Sonia originally had only one scene, but they asked to be given more to do, so I wrote in two more scenes which told us much more about them and their lives. In the original script the PC and the WPC had a bit of romance going. They even began to have a cuddle on stage. The actors who were playing these parts felt that it was too unlikely that the police would carry on in this way, so I cut the

cuddles and replaced them with the section where the WPC gets
something in her eye.

On the whole, the play had audiences made up of the people I had
written the play for and they seemed to enjoy it. One night, though,
the National Front sent a contingent of their supporters to see the
play and cause a disturbance. Whenever Spratchett made a racist
remark they cheered. They almost succeeded in ruining the
performance because there was a large group of young black people
in the audience as well, who became extremely angry. However, when
Spratchett broke down in the night scene, and then came on in a
wheelchair, the National Front group found it more difficult to cheer
and had to sit and watch the last part of the play in silence.

Andrew Bethell

FOLLOW-UP ACTIVITIES

Casting the play

Before a play can be put on stage the director has to cast the parts.
He needs to find actors who look right, sound right and will be
able to understand how that character feels. A director cannot have
a fixed idea of how the part will be interpreted because each
individual actor will bring his or her individual interpretation.
However, it is still essential that the director has a clear idea of the
kind of actor he is looking for.

For example, the first director of *Roots, Rules and Tribulation* wrote
notes on each of the characters before he began to cast the play.
This is what he wrote about Ethel:

ETHEL: A tramp now, although she once lived a very
different life. She can still show signs of her
original elegance, so her voice and accent should
be semi-refined.

She will have to be strong at certain points in
the play and she holds her own against Spratchett.
The more loony bits must not be overdone, so the
part needs a sensitive actress.

She must be able to move like an old person,
even if her voice sounds younger.

A bit like Edna in *Edna the Inebriate Woman*.

Imagine you are the director of a production of *Roots*. Write casting notes on the following characters:

Spratchet	Mrs Walton
Reg	Denise
Pete	Ethel
Norris	Maggie

Your notes should show what you think the character is like; what he or she looks like; what sort of voice or accent he or she will have.

It is sometimes helpful to think of examples of the kind of person you mean from among people or actors you already know. They could be people in your school or actors you have seen on television.

Designing the play

In its first production *Roots* was presented on stage with the audience on three sides of it. The set looked like this:

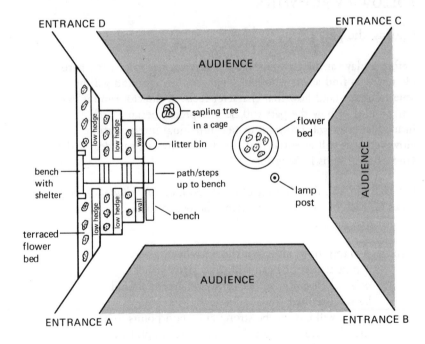

Here are two other theatre plans.

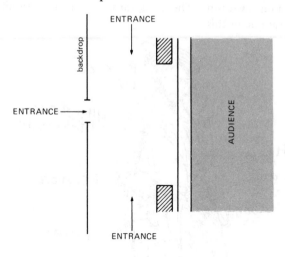

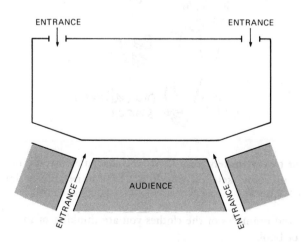

Can you design a set for *Roots* to fit one of these theatres? If you have a
theatre, stage or drama room in your school, design a set to fit your
space.

Designing the costumes

Here is how the costume designer working on *Roots* planned Ethel's
costume. She has drawn a picture of what she was hoping Ethel might
look like. She also wrote some notes about the effect she was trying to
achieve and the details.

It is very often the small details that make a costume 'work', especially for plays set in our own time. The dying carnation in the buttonhole is an excellent example of this.

Select one or two characters from *Roots* and design a costume for each. Try to make up some sketches, you do not have to be able to draw, although it helps.

You could find examples of the clothes you are thinking of in magazines or books.

For some characters you will need to do more than one design because they change their costume during the play.

Make notes on the details: e.g. jewellery, badges, ties etc. You could include a few scraps of material to give an idea of what clothes would be made of.

If you are working on the costume designs of a real production, you will need to give some ideas as to where the clothes might come from.

Editing and cutting

A play is not like a novel, which is completely finished and unchangeable when it is printed. Because a play has to be interpreted by the director and the actors, it is always changing. A play-script is a working document and the writer, the director and the actors all have a right to change it if they really think it necessary.

Here is a page from the original script of *Roots* after the director had made his changes:

W.P.C.:   Can you tell us what it's about. It might help.

Man: He was one of them. One of those... animals, that did it.

W.P.C.:   Did what?

Man: To my Barry. they did it. ~~He was a good boy, worked hard for us he did.~~ And they got him, on the common, just because he was different. ~~Individual he was, not one of the sheep.~~ But they ~~had to...~~ hadto...

W.P.C.:   ~~Had to what?~~ They what?

Man: Attacked him, ~~and kicked him,~~ kicked him half to death.

W.P.C.:   What? When?

Man: On the common. He was just walking and him and his gang, they attacked him. ~~Ten of them on to one.~~ ~~That's the sort of odds they like you see.~~ And they kicked and smashed him, and then ran... ~~On the common, it was not far from here.~~

W.P.C.:   When was this?

Man: Only last year, and they didn't even to go prison. Digging in a garden what sort of a punishment's that? We're the one's that's punished - looking after him. ~~He can hardly talk, sits there staring.~~ Can't walk on his own anymore. The wife's with him all the time, ~~every minute.~~ See, I wanted the revenge, for her sake as much as mine.

P.C.:   Oh God!

W.P.C.:   What?

P.C.:   I remember. The 'queer bashing' case on Winsley Common.

Man: Just because he was different you see.

Denise: Is that right?

Pete: Eh?   *Leave all this until the man is off.*

Denise: Is that right?

Pete: Kind of.

Denise: Were you on that 'queer bashing' business? He was brain damaged wasn't he? What do you mean 'kind of'?

Can you explain why the director made those changes? Has he improved the scene? What was wrong with it before he made the changes?

Are there any scenes in the play which do not sound right to you? Find a section of a scene that you think could be improved and make notes of the changes necessary.

Read your version to someone else. Does he or she agree that you have improved it?

Are there any sections of the play that you think should be cut out? Decide where your cuts would be and make notes on why you want to cut those lines out. Imagine you will have to explain to the author why you want to cut the play (he spent a lot of time and effort writing those lines, so the reasons had better be good!).

Staging the play

The director needs to plan each scene very carefully. Not only will he plan the actions and the movements, but he will also have a general view of what the scene should look like and the effect it will have on the audience.

To do this he needs to ask himself a series of questions:
(1) From which entrance will each character come and what position should he or she take up on the stage?
(2) At what points will each character move and how?
(3) Which objects and props need to be where during the scene?
(4) How can I be sure that the audience understands what is going on within the scene?
(5) How will I make the scene achieve its intended effect, e.g. funny or sad or exciting, etc?
(6) What do I expect from the actors in this scene?

Here is a page from the director's script:

[handwritten: from Entrance (4)]   *[handwritten: wheels it to flowerbed.]*

(Enter <u>Ethel</u>. She is a tramp whose life is conducted in an imaginary set of relationships based on half recalled memories and the rubbish she collects and carried with her in a portable shopping trolley. She is looking) *[handwritten: to rubbish bin]*

Ethel: Now where is it? I'm sure I've put it somewhere obvious. I'll try my desk again, it could have slipped down behind the <u>Readers Digest</u> books. (She rootles through the rubbish bin)

Reg: Morning Ethel. How's things with you? *[handwritten: Carries on working]*

Ethel: Ah yes, I was going to show you that letter from my son in Adelaide. Such a nice one this week, so full of news.

[handwritten: up the steps] (She moves towards Reg. He knows the routine and goes on digging)

Would you just hold this for me while I find it.

Reg: Not just now Ethel, I'm busy. *[handwritten: gentle but firm]*

Ethel: Just for a moment please. I won't be a moment. If you could just hold these papers, I could find the letter.

Reg: (firm) No! You can read me the letter when you find it.

Ethel: (Rumaging) It's here somewhere. I won't be long Enid, I'll have that bath after you, I'm just... *[handwritten: plenty of rubbish on the floor]*

(Muttering she begins to unload her basket - room for improvisation).

[handwritten: from Entrance (1)] (Enter <u>Spratchett</u> he is behaving like an N.C.O. in charge of a group of recruits and not being deterred by the lack of any recognizable order in the recipients: <u>Pete</u>, <u>Sidney</u>, <u>Carlton</u>, <u>Denise</u>, <u>Arlene</u>, <u>Jo</u>)

Spratchett: Keep to the path, step up now. No dawdling. You're on the firm's time now. *[handwritten: standing to attention]*

(Jo goes to investigate a plant) *[handwritten: to left of flower bed.]*

ON THE PATH! I said. Leave that alone, it's still alive it doesn't need any help from you.

(The group sidle on. Sullen oblivious. Dressed in shapeless but newish overalls. Reg watches leaning on a <u>fork</u>. Carlton is talking to Arlene at the back).

Come along there Sambo, we haven't got all day. Not like where you come from. And you young lady, you should know better.

Arlene: Are you going to take that Sambo shit.

Carlton: It's nothing new, just genetic insecurity.

Spratchett: I'm going to ignore that. *[handwritten: Denise must get in close here]*

Denise: You'll have to won't you, 'cos you don't know what it means.

(She has her overalls unbuttoned low in the front).

Spratchett: Now just button yourself up girl. I can see far too much.

Denise: Like it do you? *[handwritten: sets off up the steps to bench]*

Spratchett: Now don't arouse me young lady.

Denise: I'm not a miracle worker. Is this the garden then or does this route march carry on for ever? *[handwritten: By this time Jo must be on the lawn.]*

Pick one of the scenes or incidents listed below and work out how you would stage it on the set you have designed. (If you have not designed a set, look back at page 82 and use the drawing of the original stage plan.)

Practise making notes like those on the page above.

(1) The episode where Spratchett catches Carlton and Arlene kissing (pages 45-47).
(2) The arrest (pages 29-31).

(3) Act Two, Scene 2: the scene in the dark with Spratchett and Ethel (pages 53-6).

(4) Act Three, Scene 1: the scene when those in the park react to the climax of the siege. Begin with Donald's and Susie's entrance (pages 73-6).

Questions asked by the cast

During the rehearsals the play will be discussed in great depth by the actors and the director. The director is expected to have an opinion on most aspects of the play and will have to answer many of the questions asked by the actors.

Here are some of the questions asked by the actors working on *Roots*. How would you have answered them if you were the director?

Spratchett

'I am worried that he doesn't sound very realistic in the first part of the play. I don't think people like him exist. How should I act those first scenes?'

'When I surprise Arlene and Carlton on page 47 why am I so upset?'

'I think I understand why he breaks down at the end of Act Two, Scene 2, but what's all that about the army? Why is he saying all that?'

'I still don't understand what my relationship with Ethel is. Why don't I just have her put away?'

'How much have I changed by the third act? I know I am in a wheelchair, but should I act differently from the way I do in Acts Two and Three?'

Nigel

'I really don't think that I would put up with Spratchett. Why haven't I got out of the job a long time ago?'

'What is my attitude to the young offenders and the punishment they are receiving?'

'Once I become acting park keeper how should I show I am behaving differently?'

Carlton

'I am not sure what Carlton was put away for. He doesn't seem to be much of a villain. What do you think he has done?'

Arlene

'What exactly is my relationship with my father? It seems to change all the time.'

Denise

'I am not happy with this "stupid bird" idea. Isn't there more to Denise than someone who flirts with the boys and then gets herself pregnant?'

If you were given one of the following parts, can you think of the questions you might ask the director?

Pete	**Mrs Walton**
Norris	**Jo**
Police Constable	**Doreen**

When you have worked out the questions you could give them to someone else who could try to answer them.

Writing about the play

All the exercises on the previous pages have concentrated on the process of presenting this play to an audience. Anyone who has worked on all these exercises is sure to have considered the play in considerable depth. Any of these exercises could provide the basis for a longer piece of writing.

In school, however, it is often necessary to produce a longer piece of critical writing because that is the kind of writing examiners will be interested in. Here are five essay titles on which to base a formal piece of writing about the play:

(1) *Roots, Rules and Tribulation* is a play about punishment. Many different attitudes to punishment are expressed and represented. Describe how the main characters in the play feel about punishment and decide whether you think the writer is sympathetic to the idea of community homes and community service projects or not.

(2) 'People like Spratchett just do not exist. By putting him on stage,

saying what he does, you are merely encouraging people to think like him.'

Do you agree with this statement? How realistic is Spratchett, and do you think it is right to have someone on stage saying the kind of things he says?

(3) How does the play treat black people and the problems they face living in Britain today? Do you think they are realistic characters or are they merely stereotyped characters in unreal situations?

(4) 'This play would have been much better if the writer had concentrated on the main characters and left out all the extra scenes with truants, policemen and joggers, etc.'

Do you agree? How do you think the author would justify the various sub-plots? What do you think they add to the play?

(5) Is *Roots, Rules and Tribulation* an optimistic or a pessimistic play?